How to Effectively Market Your Personal Injury Law Practice in the 21st Century

And Compete With the Mega Firms

SECOND EDITION

By Kenneth L. Hardison

PILMMA Publishing
607 Briarwood Drive, Suite 4
Myrtle Beach, SC 29572

ACKNOWLEDGEMENTS

I want to thank everyone who helped me with writing this book. There are too many to specifically recognize, but I'd like to mention a few for without whom this book would not exist.

Valerie Beasley for all her help with editing and feedback; Dale Tincher and Gerry Oginski for contributing chapters to make this edition even better than the first.

I would also like to thank Trey Ryder, Dan Kennedy, and Jay Abraham for their invaluable mentorship and sharing with me their priceless knowledge of marketing and advertising.

TABLE OF CONTENTS

INTRODUCTION

It's hard to believe that four years have passed since I wrote the first edition of this book. There have been several changes in how law firms market their practices since 2009.

For the most part, only technology has drastically changed. There are many new opportunities for lawyers to market their firms and get more leads at a better ROI (return on investment) due to new technology.

The Personal Injury and Disability lawyers who refuse to change with the times are becoming extinct. They cannot survive with all the new competition from firms who have actively started marketing their services.

The Internet and digital media has changed the landscape of the market. For the first time more consumers are using the Internet than watching T.V. Big T.V. advertisers are spending more and more each year to try to squeeze out the less relevant spenders.

Smart lawyers are using media to combat these big T.V. advertisers. In addition, the market leaders are embracing new technology and online marketing tactics.

I have addressed these new online strategies and to be honest, that part of the book will probably be outdated within a year. But, the majority of what I am going to share with you are basic principles of marketing that will never change. The media you use to implement them is the only change you can expect.

I know you will find this book helpful and I hope you see your practice grow exponentially by implementing some of the tactics discussed here. If something truly resonates with you and you actively see an increased ROI thanks to the implementation of something you read in this book, let me know. Email me at ken@pilmma.org. I'd love to hear about your success and help in any way I can.

Dedicated to your success,

Kenneth L. Hardison

PART ONE:

THE BASIC PRINCIPLES OF MARKETING

CHAPTER 1:

Marketing vs. Advertising
What's The Difference?

Before you can sell your legal services to anyone else, you have to sell them to yourself. Unless you can pinpoint what makes your law firm unique in a world of homogenous competitors, you cannot target your marketing efforts successfully.

Most lawyers make a critical mistake by confusing advertising with marketing. Marketing is "how clients and potential clients perceive your law firm." Advertising is simply "one of the many ways you can market your firm." In other words, if marketing is a wheel, advertising is one of many spokes of that wheel.

MODERN MARKETING

WHEEL

@joe_wallace SOCIAL DEVIANTS

Understanding the difference between advertising and marketing is a critical step in developing a strategic plan for a law firm. By using both terms interchangeably, many lawyers confuse "marketing their firm" with "advertising their firm." Ignoring these differences can negatively impact the outcome of your marketing plan.

As mentioned above, advertising is just one element of your marketing plan. Also, it is the most expensive way to market your firm -- and the most difficult way to track. That said, you must incorporate other tactics to market your practice.

2

Remember -- TV, Yellow Pages, and websites are all ways of advertising your firm. But, there are infinite ways to market your firm in addition to advertising. I will discuss these ways in the following sections of this book.

Market Research

Buying a fishing pole and worms, then dropping the line into a lake, is like advertising. But being the fisherman who researches what types of fish live in the lake, the best bait to use, what the water temperature is, the water depth, the typical weather at the lake, and when the moon will be full, is like marketing.

You must think like the fish. What the fish likes and what you like are different. The same bait that would attract you, will not attract the fish. Same with potential clients – you are not your client.

Like the example above, law firms should include the same type of in-depth research before creating a marketing plan. It took me a while to truly understand this, but once I did, the cases started flowing in like a river of salmon swimming to their spawning grounds.

When I was trying to figure out the positioning statement for my firm, I contacted past clients who had referred others to the firm. I wanted to figure out exactly what I did to leave such an impression that they would refer others to my practice. My perception was that a case's positive outcome will be the ultimate deciding factor for a client to be satisfied enough to refer more clients.

The results of my research shocked me. While a positive outcome of the case was important, my firm's dedication to client service was the primary reason they referred others. While this may not be the case for your firm, I found that whether a case was settled in favor of a client was not the primary factor in deciding the level of client satisfaction. It came down to how well the client was treated.

Practical Advice. Proven Solutions.
www.PILMMA.org

Let's face it, people hire lawyers they know, like and trust. They also refer people to lawyers they know, like and trust. By giving exceptional client service, our existing and past clients refer us a boatload of cases. Why? Because they know, like and trust us!

Once I had the results from my research, I wanted to create a positioning statement that would emphasize my firm's dedication to client satisfaction in all of my marketing. While other firms make unrealistic promises of "big settlements," I want to make promises I know I can keep.

After brainstorming with my partner, associates, and staff, we concluded that our positioning statement must imply two things:

1) We provide exceptional legal service, and

2) We provide the highest level of client service.

Thus, our marketing plan includes marketing systems and advertising methods that allow our firm to convey this message. We communicate this message clearly in the tagline, "Putting You First".

We have implemented this in a variety of ways. We have a Client Bill of Rights, a 24/7 Client Advocate Hotline, and a 100% Client Satisfaction Guarantee (see www.LawyerNC.com). All of our advertising also conveys this message. We have never said, "We get the largest verdicts or settlements in every case." To promise something that is impossible to guarantee is deceiving. Our only promise is exceptional client service and that the client will always come first.

My point is, without thorough research, you will not understand your clients or what made them choose you or refer people to you. And, as with any marketing plan, market research should be a major priority. Without it, you're really just dropping a line into a lake, hoping that a fish will bite. One way to conduct this research, or at least get started, is a SWOT Analysis.

Practical Advice. Proven Solutions.
www.PILMMA.org

SWOT ANALYSIS & CHART

When contemplating your marketing strategy, one of the most effective tools to use for finding your way is the SWOT Analysis. A SWOT analysis is commonly used in marketing and business to identify positive and negative elements that may affect any new efforts. An acronym for Strengths, Weaknesses, Opportunities and Threats, this analysis will push you to really think about your law firm and your next steps in a strategic yet tactical manner. There may be some things you don't realize about your firm or the direction in which you're heading, or the place you're in for that matter. This exercise will flush it all out for you.

Although it sounds easy, most law firm owners don't know how to properly use a SWOT analysis to guide their businesses Think about it this way – it's all about leveraging your strengths, outsourcing and partnering where you are weak, focusing on opportunities and being aware of threats. When you put it like that, it really is quite simple. The hard part is actually doing it.

The SWOT analysis enables you to identify the positive and negative influencing factors inside and outside of your law firm. The key role of SWOT is to help develop a full awareness of all factors that may affect strategic planning and decision making.

A good SWOT analysis serves as a dashboard to your legal services and when done correctly can help you navigate and implement a sound marketing and management strategy for your firm regardless of your size.

A SWOT analysis focuses entirely on the four elements included in the acronym, allowing you to identify the forces influencing a strategy, action or initiative. Knowing these positive and negative impacting elements can help you more effectively communicate what elements of your plan need to be recognized.

When drafting a SWOT analysis, include a table, split into four columns so as to list each impacting element side-by-side

Practical Advice. Proven Solutions.
www.PILMMA.org

for comparison. (I've included one for you.) Strengths and weaknesses won't typically match the opportunities and threats listed, although some correlation should exist since they are tied together in some way.

Once you've identified your risks, you can then decide whether it is most appropriate to eliminate the internal weaknesses by assigning company resources to fix the problems or reduce the external threats by abandoning the threatened area of business.

The first two letters of the acronym, Strengths and Weaknesses, refer to internal factors, meaning the resources and experiences readily available to you and your firm. These typically include:

- Financial resources – funding, income, investments
- Physical resources – location, facilities, equipment
- Human resources – employees, volunteers, target audience, etc.
- Current processes – employee programs, departments, software systems

When it comes to listing strengths and weaknesses, you shouldn't try to sugarcoat or glaze over inherent weaknesses or strengths. You must be brutally honest with your employees, your partners and most importantly, yourself.

Every law firm and individual is influenced and affected by external forces. Whether connected directly or indirectly to an opportunity or threat, each of these factors is important to take note of and document. External factors include things you and your firm do not control, typically:

- Market trends – new products, services, technology or shifts in audience needs/desires
- Economic trends – local, national and international financial trends
- Funding – donations, legislature, and other foundations
- Demographics – target audience's age, race, gender and culture

As I mentioned before, I've included a sample for you here. After the sample template, you'll see another with some examples filled in for you.

SWOT Analysis Template

Internal	
Strengths	Weaknesses
1.	1.

External	
Opportunities	Threats
1.	1.

SWOT Analysis Summary

Practical Advice. Proven Solutions.
www.PILMMA.org

Strengths	Weaknesses
• Political support • Funding available • Market experience • Strong leadership	• Project is very complex • Likely to be costly • May have an environmental impact • Staff resources are already stretched
Opportunities	**Threats**
• Project may improve local economy • Will improve safety • Project will boost firm's public image	• Environmental constraints • Time delays • Opposition to change

The SWOT analysis is a simple, but comprehensive strategy for identifying not only the weaknesses and threats of a plan, but also the strengths and opportunities available through it. While it's an excellent brainstorming tool, this four-cornered analysis will prompt you to examine and execute strategies in a more balanced way. When used in conjunction with other analysis models, these frameworks for strategic thinking are well worth your time and should guide your decision making.

Which brings me to another important point that lawyers must understand and implement in order for their marketing and advertising to be successful – ***you must differentiate yourself from your competitors!***

CHAPTER 2:

Why A Unique Selling Proposition Is Vital To Any Marketing Campaign

Imitation may be the sincerest form of flattery but when it comes to marketing your law firm and beating your competition, it falls flat. A large majority of lawyers assume that copying their competitors' ads will help them compete with them. Don't fall into this trap. This is ineffective, costly and gives you and your law firm no competitive advantage in the marketplace whatsoever. In 1961, Rosser Reeves wrote a book called "Reality in Advertising" that literally revolutionized the marketing industry. The book was so influential that it became a college textbook for marketing students. In his book, Mr. Reeves announced the idea that every business, product, or service absolutely must have a "USP" or a "Unique Selling Proposition". He maintained that focusing on the USP in every advertising and marketing effort was key to creating an effective and cohesive advertising and marketing campaign.

What is a USP?

A USP is a compelling marketing message that dramatically sets you apart from your competitors and boldly broadcasts the unique benefits your legal services provide. It's the number one benefit or total of all benefits that differentiates you and your law firm from all other law firms in your market.

Simply put a USP is:

- An overt, unique claim about your law firm or a promise of benefits of your legal services.
- A statement that impressively positions you as distinctly different from your competitors.
- A statement that is so strong, attractive and compelling that it motivates prospects to choose you over all other firms.

Basically, a USP is a distinct, compelling statement about the difference that separates you apart from your competitors and answers this basic question – *Why should I do business with your law firm rather than with your competitors or better yet why should I hire a lawyer at all?*

Why do you need a USP?

You need a USP because your potential prospects are getting hammered every day with hundreds of ads from your competitors! They all say the same things, "We're tough and aggressive", "We care", "Free Consultation", "We don't get paid unless we win". These ads clutter the airwaves and have consumers' heads spinning with everyone saying the same thing. No wonder prospective clients don't know who to hire - no one stands out! How can a prospective client choose the law firm that's right for them when they all look the same, sound the same and make all the same promises? The fact that the legal advertising space is cluttered with cookie cutter ads and the same messages over and over is actually a good thing for you. This gives you a golden opportunity to stand out from your competition. How do you do this? You get a USP. Now.

This is your opportunity to stand out from the crowd.

How to Develop Your Firm's USP

Most lawyers I talk to say *"Ken, we do all the same things our competitors are doing"*, *"We are bound by laws and regulations on what we can do and what we can say to potential clients"*, *"We don't have much choice, there really is no way to stand out from the crowd"*.

My answer to that is simply, this - it can be done. Is it easy? Not necessarily, but with the right mindset and tools, you can create a USP for your firm that will increase the return on your investment (ROI) from your advertising three to ten times what it presently yields.

Practical Advice. Proven Solutions.
www.PILMMA.org

To develop a powerful and effective USP, you must think like a potential client. What keeps them up at night? What is their big problem you can solve? What is the headache your firm can cure? Above all else, focus on answering the potential client's most critical question, *"What's in it for me?"* The only way to answer that question is to sell the "benefits" of your law firm and not the "features" of your legal services.

What's the different between a benefit and a feature? Take the eraser on a pencil for example. The feature of that eraser is that is will erase your mistakes. The eraser benefits you by saving you time and effort by not requiring you to rewrite everything from the beginning if you make a mistake. The benefit is the time you save. See the difference?

How about a benefit versus a feature in action in a USP? Let's take Domino's Pizza. They advertise *"Piping Hot Pizza Delivered in 30 minutes or less..."* The benefit is hot, instead of cold, pizza and fast, instead of slow, delivery. By focusing on the benefits, they are showing the consumers what's in it for them. Every consumer now knows if you order Domino's, you'll get hot pizza delivered fast. This is how Domino's differentiated themselves from the other competitors in the pizza delivery business and created a multi-million dollar business. NOTE – Domino's never claimed to be the best tasting pizza. They focused on their target market - people who want and need pizza fast and cheap. Focus on your prospective clients. Your USP should tell them that you're the firm that can give it to them better than any other. This is key. You must know what your prospective clients want in order to create a USP that works.

Why do people resist hiring a lawyer? Many do so because they lack funds and are afraid they will be taken advantage of. I used this fear to create the USP for my SSD law firm. We use a *"30 Day Client Service Satisfaction Guarantee – No questions and no fees."* We give new clients the opportunity to try our firm for 30 days. At anytime during the first 30 Days, they aren't completely 100%

satisfied with the way we treat them and their case, they can ask for their file back with no fees. See www.CarolinaSSDLawyers.com.

While it's a compelling offer in-and-of-itself, the benefit to the potential client is that they can "try us" and change lawyers without the fear of having to pay for two lawyers if they aren't 100% happy. In our USP, I incorporated the concept of risk reversal. By giving them a 30 Day Guarantee with no fees, we take all of the risk, leaving the client able and willing to take action risk-free. The benefit, again, is that they are not stuck with a law firm they are not happy with.

As stated earlier, most lawyers say, *"We all do the same things and are constrained by rules and regulations so our hands are tied."* I disagree. What you do may be the same, but how you do it is a different question altogether. You could have a "Client Bill of Rights" or a Client Advocate…You could offer to handle property damage for free…All these things could be molded into your USP.

A Preemptive USP

You could be the first lawyer in your market to promote a particular benefit that all other lawyers in your market similarly provide or offer. Because everyone else provides it or is doing it, no one bothers to promote it. Why is this? Why would you not promote something that would cause a prospective client to hire you? So what if everyone else does it? If no one is promoting it, you should be the first to shout it from the rooftops! If no one is talking about it, how do potential clients know you're doing it? Let it set you apart. This is called creating a preemptive USP.

In other words, you are promoting the facts of what you do. And even though all the other lawyers do the same thing, you will have given yourself a competitive advantage simply by stating it. If you say it first, you'll establish a preeminent market position and will perceived as the market leader. Other firms who try to follow suit and quickly claim the same thing will be considered "copycats" and "me too" firms and will only end up advertising you.

For example if you began advertising your USP as *"We will handle your P.P. or Med Pay Claim for free"*, even if every other lawyer in town does it, you are the first to use it to differentiate the way you handle a case. This is how you execute a preemptive USP.

There are three main ways to develop your firm's USP. The first is the Garry Halbert Index Card Shuffle. This is where you list your firm's features on one side of a card and turn each feature into a benefit on the other side. You rank and score them in order of importance and from there you get your sticking points for your USP. That method is a solitary method, whereas it only involves your firm.

The other two methods are where you get your clients involved. After all, who better to tell you what's great about your firm than those you've worked with successfully? You can do this in two ways. Frustration vs. Satisfaction, leads you to a "What's the thing you hate most about lawyers?" discussion. You find out what they hate, describe that you're not like the others and there you have it – you're able to give them what they want simply because you know what they don't want! Lastly, there's the possible hidden USP. You may already have one and don't know it – so ask your clients, why they chose you. Have them tell you what it is about you and your firm that they found appealing and use it to your advantage. I go into more detail about all this in my USP Workshop, so for a detailed guide on how to do this, visit: www.CreateAUSP.com.

The key thing to remember in developing and using a USP is this: You can't be all things to all people. Select your USP and stick with it! You should use it in everything you do to market your firm. It should become your mantra -- and you should market the hell out of it! It is, after all, who you are.

CHAPTER 3:

Strategies vs. Tactics

15

Practical Advice. Proven Solutions.
www.PILMMA.org

Now that I've explained why a USP is vital to your firm's success, I want to address how to put it to use.

One of my personal favorite strategies is Jay Abraham's Strategy of Preeminence. I wholeheartedly believe in it. And while the strategy of preeminence is one upon which many great businesses and law firms have been built, if it wasn't for the tactics they used to achieve their goals, they would've never gotten to the top of their games. If you want to be the leading firm in your market, not only do you have to have a USP, but you have to understand the difference between marketing and advertising and you have to understand the difference between strategies and tactics.

You want to be the preeminent law firm in your market. You want to become your prospective clients' trusted legal advisor. Why? Because people hire lawyers they know, like and trust. Now, your goal here is to create a relationship with your target client that is nurtured to the point that you undoubtedly become their trusted legal advisor. Your goal is part of your strategy. Your tactics are what you will do – actions you will take to achieve your goal. Like I mentioned in Chapter 1 – while marketing is the wheel, advertising can be considered the spokes of the wheel – strategy is the wheel, tactics are the spokes..

How are you going to reach your goal of becoming your target clients' trusted legal advisor? You're going to exceed their expectations. Under promise and over deliver. Provide exceptional client service. Everything you do matters when it comes to reaching this goal. Every action you take can be looked at as a tactic used to achieve a particular goal within your overall strategy.

You know the old saying, "A goal without a plan is just a dream." There are few statements that ring so true. If you don't have a plan, your goals don't matter and neither does what you're doing. You have to be able to look at the big picture while still understanding the moving parts and their purposes.

Practical Advice. Proven Solutions.
www.PILMMA.org

- Strategy – Preeminence
- Goal - Become the Trusted Legal Advisor
- Tactics –
    o Develop a USP,
    o Use USP in every ad and marketing piece;
    o Newsletters;
    o Follow-up sequences,
    o Auto-responders,
    o Exceptional client service,
    o etc, etc, etc…

To put it plainly, strategy is an idea. A conceptualization of how the goal should be achieved – the big picture. A tactic is any action you take to execute the strategy and ultimately achieve your goal.

What is your marketing strategy? Do you have one?

All businesses, and in this marketplace, law firms especially, need to have a marketing strategy. All good marketing strategies share some common components:

1) A thorough understanding of you, your brand, your story – Who are you? What do you stand for? How do you want your firm to be perceived? How is it currently perceived?

2) A realistic assessment of your product/services and the strengths and weaknesses of both. You must conduct some sort of market research along with an analysis of your current state of union in order to determine the strategy most suitable for your firm.

3) A clear picture of the competition – Who is your competition? Are they getting more cases than you? Why? How are you different? What is your USP? STAND OUT!

4) Intimate knowledge of your ideal client and market – If you don't know who you serve, who you want to serve, what their options are and what they really want – everything you do is in vain.

5) A grasp of the big picture implications – How will this affect the firm overall? Bottom line? Brand? Infrastructure? Staff? Future?

Once you get your strategy together and know the goal you're working toward, you can figure out what tactics you need in order to move forward. One thing to remember is that a great strategy doesn't have to depend on remarkable tactics in order to be successful…you just have to execute everything effectively. That's the kicker here. As I've said before and I will say again, I'm an idea guy, NOT an implementer. This is where you have to be honest with yourself about your strengths and weaknesses. Bring in your team, your partner, a trusted advisor, discuss your ideas with fellow attorneys not in your market, do your SWOT Analysis….basically, be prepared. Be diligent. Know what you want, figure out how to get it and make it happen.

Practical Advice. Proven Solutions.
www.PILMMA.org

CHAPTER 4:

Direct Response vs. Brand Marketing: What Is the Difference and Why Does It Matter?

Direct response is a form of marketing designed to get an immediate response from your prospective clients. It includes a "call to action," Which directs and urges your target prospect to take a specific action or response. For example, a TV ad that says, "If you've been injured, call us right now!" Or, "Call today and talk to a lawyer the same day." Smart firms track the responses to these ads in terms of cases they accept from the number of calls/ intakes they receive following the ad.

You can track the calls from these ads by advertising a telephone number in the ads that is different from your general office number used to call your firm. Any calls to that separate number are a result of that ad. Or, you can simply ask each new caller how they heard about your firm.

Brand marketing wants to get the future potential client to "recall" the firm's name. The goal of branding is to create "top of mind awareness" and instant recall when someone is asked who they would call if they were ever injured in an automobile accident (instant recall). This is what Pepsi and Coke have done so well. They've developed such a stronghold on the soft drink market, most people will think of either one or the other when they want a soda.

The very first TV advertisements by lawyers following the Bates decision were for the most part branding messages. They focused on an "image building" marketing campaign. Today, the trend has shifted towards direct response TV ads.

The first thing most marketing experts tell you to do is brand yourself – i.e. "introduce" yourself to your audience. Once you have successfully gotten the premier position in their minds, then you can "tell them what to do" by proceeding with a direct response advertising campaign.

This takes too much time and money. By waiting until you get the premier position in their minds to go for direct response ads, you waste valuable time and effort. Coke and Pepsi can do it – you can't.

I believe that this strategy is dying and will continue to dwindle. The reason for this is simple. Today, with the power of the Internet behind law firms, branding and direct response are becoming more and more symbiotic. It will soon become the state of TV ads that branding and direct response spots will be one-and-the-same.

Most law firms use direct response in all forms of their ads -- TV, radio, and Internet. They also use their websites to provide branding images and marketing, while using direct response techniques such as "Click to Call", "Live Chat" and "Quick Contact Forms".

Successful law firms market to their target audience, and spend their money on multi-level campaigns that include direct response marketing, which allows their brand to develop while making money from an increased case load.

Practical Advice. Proven Solutions.
www.PILMMA.org

CHAPTER 5:

Consumer-Based Marketing

Today's consumers demand convenience and quality in every facet of their busy lives. Law firms that respond to the demand for high quality with high quantity, informative and personalized service will be the ones that prosper in the 21st century. As I have already mentioned, providing your "consumers" with information is the first step in becoming consumer-based, or for our sake, client-based. The next equally important step is creating an exceptional client experience. This means regularly updating the client about the progress of their case, returning their calls promptly, and so on.

It is important that, as a law firm, you always under promise and over deliver in the areas of legal service and client service. The key to this is communication. Open and honest communication about everything involved in a client's case is crucial.

The essential piece of communication that lawyers most often forget is client feedback. It is important to hear the positive things that you and your firm are doing well so you continue to do them. But, it is even more important to hear the negative feedback about what you aren't doing well.

A good avenue for this open and honest communication is a 24/7 Client Advocate Hotline. This "hotline" allows your clients to contact an "impartial" third party who can listen to them when things aren't moving forward in the manner they had anticipated. This person can hear their thoughts and concerns and help get their case back on track. This allows your firm to "under promise and over deliver" by always meeting and exceeding your client's expectations. Another avenue through which you can get honest feedback is conducting client surveys while their case is proceeding and then again at the case's conclusion.

Consumer-based law firms also use Client Service Satisfaction Guarantees. This is a guarantee that clients will be satisfied with your client service, and NOT a guarantee about the outcome of the case. No lawyer can ethically guarantee results, but they can guarantee exceptional client service.

And for the lawyers who say, "We can't give our clients a guarantee, it's just not possible." -- my response is, "If you can't and you don't -- you will become engulfed and eliminated from the market by the firms who can and will."

It isn't that hard to set-up a guarantee that supports your consumer-based focus. Find a benefit that your firm offers and then guarantee it! If you want to thrive in the 21st century, you must become consumer focused. And giving great legal service isn't enough. You must also give exceptional client service!

Practical Advice. Proven Solutions.
www.PILMMA.org

CHAPTER 6:

How to Create Trust By Educating Your Prospective Clients

Consumers are "hip" to the attorney ads that promise the biggest settlements. They are tired of the high pressure sales tactics that lawyers use to try to gain their business. They are skeptical about doing business based on these huge, unrealistic promises made during blatant sales driven tactics.

Clients are consumers. I know that goes without saying, but we often forget what this really means. If we are going to successfully generate clients, we must understand today's consumer. And, today's consumer is about "me!" "What can you do for 'me'?"

It doesn't matter what law school you attended or what your biggest case was. They want to know what _you_ can do for **them**.

Understanding what the client wants is crucial because the client's needs change as their case progresses. And, before they hire a lawyer, they first need INFORMATION.

They want as much information about their case as they can get. Many times, this will result in them getting legal advice from a friend, family member, or a message board online. These are the last places we want prospective clients to get legal advice. After all, we are the legal authority in their area. We want prospective clients to come to us for all of the legal information they need. And undoubtedly, this will lead to them hiring us.

We have to remember, prospective clients have the exact needs and wants that all consumers have. This includes the need for information, which all consumers want before making a purchase decision. They want to be informed!

The best way to make sure that you're the one supplying this desired information is through education-based marketing. As lawyers, we must change our image and the way we get our marketing message to prospective clients. We are the public's most reliable source of legal information. We must convey that in our marketing efforts.

Remember, you're in a race to get those prospective clients before your competitors do. Doesn't it make sense that you should be the lawyer who's supplying them with their desired information before they decide to hire an attorney? That's why I encourage you to engage these consumers and give them the valuable information they want and need.

According to legal marketing advisor Trey Ryder, education-based marketing is built around an educational message that replaces the usual sales message lawyers typically use. The educational message is commonly delivered to prospective clients through educational means like reports, white papers, books, newsletters, videos, DVDs, CDs, and the Internet.

Instead of using a sales pitch like, "We'll get you more money," or "Show them you mean business," you use education as an incentive to get prospective clients to read your information. For example, "*9 Common Mistakes That Can Ruin Your Disability Claim*" can be the title of a short book or report that you can offer prospective clients who are in the process of filing for Social Security Disability.

Once you create the informational product, offer it to prospects for free. Do this through paid advertising in TV, radio, newspapers, and on websites. You can also offer it in your newsletter. Once the prospect sees the ad offering the free information, they will call your office, and at least 25% of the time they will hire you on that initial contact.

But the best part is, you earn your prospective client's trust because you've already made an effort to help them regardless of whether they hire you.

My firm has created four books, two booklets, and three different reports to support our education-based marketing campaign. Every time my firm gets a first-time caller who has been in an auto accident and is shopping for a lawyer, the caller is put

Practical Advice. Proven Solutions.
www.PILMMA.org

through an aggressive, yet dignified, follow-up process that focuses on our educational marketing material. These callers need a lawyer immediately, and it's important to follow-up quickly and effectively before they choose one of your competitors.

- **Day 1**- The day they call, I send a letter thanking them for showing interest in my firm. Along with the letter, I include an informational book I wrote about legal matters concerning auto accidents and property damage. I also add their information to my firm's newsletter mailing list.

- **Day 3**- I send out a free report, *"The 29 Tactics Adjusters Use to Deny Your Claim."*

- **Day 6**- I send out another free report, *"59 Legal Defenses the Insurance Adjusters Use to Diminish Your Claim."*

- **Day 9**- I send out a book I wrote on *"How to Handle Property Damage"*.

The key is to create content-rich material that helps the prospective client. You also want a good title to arouse curiosity and interest for their given case. My firm's book for the Social Security practice is titled *"The 7 Costly Mistakes That Can Ruin Your Social Security Disability Claim"*. For Personal Injury cases we have *"The 7 Fatal Mistakes That Victims of Accidents Make in N.C. and How to Avoid Making them."*

Inside the books we cover the common myths and misconceptions the public has about their type of case. We also include a section on frequently asked questions and definitions to educate the reader on the subject matter.

These books are seen as "must reads" by all of my clients and prospective clients who have inquired about my firm. With these books, we are offering prospective clients something of value for free, which also fulfills their immediate need for information. And as they pass my useful educational marketing material around to friends and family members, my firm's caseload continues to increase.

There are unlimited ways you can use educational marketing materials that will also promote your firm, and yourself, as the area's authority on legal matters. Visit www.LawyerNC.com to see more examples of how you can distribute useful information to your prospective clients.

Another key advantage to education-based marketing is its ease of tracking. You will immediately know how well it is working, unlike the majority of your marketing efforts. You know how many callers are inquiring about the free informational products. And, you can offer your free material online and track how many people are signing up through your website.

Websites are an ideal method for providing this information. There are no time limitations like in TV or radio commercials and no space limitations like with billboards or Yellow Pages. People are already on the Internet 24/7 searching for one thing-- information.

Online, you are in a prime spot to provide them with the means to obtain their desired information -- instantly! Odds are, people are searching online for information about their case anyway. Who better to supply valuable and credible information than you?

Websites are also the ideal medium for offering education-based material because you can update it and change it on a daily basis. The information is as current and up-to-date as you want it to be.

And foremost, you maintain your dignity because you never have to overtly sell your service -- for which your prospective clients are most grateful!

We are and always have been in the service industry. The key to getting more clients is to embrace this concept by becoming consumer-based law firms. In doing this you provide

29

"consumers" with useful information and education that will better their understanding of their case and the legal system. By focusing on this you accomplish several things:

1) You position yourself as the expert

2) You provide goodwill and positive community relations

3) You help bolster your image in your market area

4) You create "reciprocity" – by giving them what they're asking for– information. And, they will give you what you want-- their business

5) You establish credibility and make a positive first impression by offering helpful information rather than a sales pitch.

6) You create trust.

7) They get to know and like you.

By following the education-based marketing model described above, your firm can raise the bar on providing ethical and dignified advertising for your legal services. Give prospective clients what they are truly searching for—information!

Remember, as I stated earlier – people hire lawyers they know, like and trust. Educational materials such as books, CDs, DVDs and reports help establish all three triggers above.

PART II:

Marketing Strategies
For the 21st Century

CHAPTER 7:

Internet and Websites

The Internet is exploding in usage and popularity. Most homes have more than one computer. A high percentage of individuals have access to the Internet or know someone who does. Older consumers are using the Internet to communicate with family members. Services such as weather.com, MapQuest, eBay, Google, and others are bringing more people to the Internet. Individuals are learning that they can shop more conveniently and more affordably via the Internet. Social Media such as Facebook, Twitter and blogs are more than prevalent.

According to InternetWorldStats.com, more than 78% of the population in North America uses the Internet. And over half of all users in the world are located in North America. Any lawyer who is under the misconception that his or her clients aren't online is dead wrong!

While law firms closely analyze their Yellow Page and television advertising campaigns, more and more are moving their advertising dollars to the Internet. The web continues to report increasing returns, in large part because of the medium's ability to emphasize relevance and value.

Advertisers are cutting back on TV and print media spending in favor of ads that run alongside search listings. According to Forbes.com, online ad spending topped $100 Billion in 2012. This spending is set to increase in double digits throughout at least 2015. Digital ads now command nearly one in five ad dollars. North America alone commands 39% of all digital ad spending. It is projected that by 2016, digital ad spending will pass a quarter of all ad dollars.

All of these factors reinforce the importance of developing a strong Internet presence. If you choose the right Web consultant, you are, in effect, building the equivalent of a store front on a growing street corner that is open 24 hours per day, 7 days per week. This is obviously superior to traditional ads that run one time. Your investment today will be far less than it will be in the future when other firms discover the value of Internet marketing and jump in as competitors. In addition, your Internet investment will continue to pay dividends since it strengthens your website presence. Your annual costs will decrease in year two, and the number of potential clients will increase.

But if you wish to capitalize on the web's potential, you must prepare yourself. The Internet can work well if you approach it in the right fashion.

First Steps to Success

A good first step to preparing your online presence is to decide whether to develop your own Web staff or find an Internet provider. Jerry Parker of Parker Waichman's YourLawyer.com does an admirable job of staffing and developing his own web presence. Most firms, however, find a capable web vendor to help manage their presence. Our firm uses Consultwebs.com, but there are others that focus on law firm marketing, including The Search Engine Guys (TSEG.com), Justia (Justia.com), SLS Consulting (SLSConsulting.com), and Everspark Interactive (eversparkinteractive.com). In my opinion, Consultwebs is the ideal company for handling any law firm's online presence.

There are three main components to being successful on the Internet.

- First, prospective clients have to find you.
- Second, your website must be compelling and informative.
- Third, your website must be set up to maximize conversions.

For a prospective client to find you, your web presence must be search engine optimized (SEO) properly, or you must purchase pay-per-click ads. Google owns about 70% of the search engine marketplace. If you SEO well for Google, you will typically do well in the other major search engines.

Why is it important to achieve high rankings? Simply put, it is because the law firms that rank in the top 10 receive virtually all of the cases. Those firms that rank in the top five listings receive a higher percentage of cases than those in the second five listings. Virtually all firms that rank at the top obtain a large quantity.

SEO is targeted for the traditional listings, usually called "organic" or free listings, as opposed to pay-per-click ads, which can be purchased. Achieving high rankings in the organic listings is not easy. Search engines periodically change the ranking algorithms or formulas that they use to rank websites. They do this for a variety of reasons, but the main reason is because they want to provide high quality results that match the user's queries.

To be successful, your SEO firm must use a multi-pronged approach that includes a variety of components: high-quality content, proper search engine meta-tag descriptors, and proper use of keywords. High-quality, relevant incoming links are also important. Search engines conclude that if a site has relevant high quality incoming links, it is well-established and provides user value.

Searching for a Search Engine Optimization Firm

Many companies claim to be able to provide high search engine rankings. But how can you verify that? Fortunately, you can easily evaluate their results by testing their clients' practice area rankings in Google to see how they rank. Do not, however, simply test a few carefully selected reference clients that are provided by the vendor.

• **Check the client list.** Hopefully, your prospective vendor will provide a client list on their website. Unfortunately, many do not. If a vendor does not list its clients, type the vendor's name

Practical Advice. Proven Solutions.
www.PILMMA.org

into Google, find several of the upper tier clients and test their rankings. It is important to test the upper tier clients because some law firms purchase design-only contracts as opposed to design and SEO.

• **Check search phrases.** Another way to test vendors is to type its targeted search phrase into Google. Try typing "law firm Web consultants", "law firm Web designers", "law firm SEO consultants", "law firm Web marketing consultants" and similar phrases into Google. If they can't achieve rankings for themselves, they are unlikely to be able to achieve rankings for you.

• **Check with clients.** Call the vendor's clients and ask if they are achieving higher rankings and receiving cases. Ask if the vendor seems to make periodic changes to improve their rankings -- or if they simply made the sale and moved on to the next customer. Ask if the firm measures the cost of their cases and if they think the return from SEO is better than their other advertising media. Ask if they think that their rankings compare favorably to their competitors' rankings.

• **Find a legal specialty vendor.** It is important that your SEO vendor be legal-specific. If they are, they will have had experience in achieving high rankings for law firms. They will probably have access to a network of legal sites that will consider linking to you if your site has value. If they also develop websites, they will be able to save you significant amounts of time since you will not have to educate them on ethics and legal content issues. It is helpful if the vendor is both legal-SEO and web design-specific. SEO firms that sell books and legal research, for example, or do dentist and doctor sites may gravitate to other areas if they make more money there. They may also apply their efforts or their best people to other areas of their business – leaving you behind.

• **Look for staying power.** SEO firms often go out of business or evolve into different types of Web companies when they cannot

Practical Advice. Proven Solutions.
www.PILMMA.org

achieve success in SEO. Find out how long your prospective or existing vendor has been in business.

• **Evaluate vendor size and skill.** Find out if your vendor is a one- or two-person firm or has multiple personnel. A small SEO firm cannot provide the amount of effort required to achieve rankings. Find out if your vendor does the work or farms it out to contractors or off-shore workers. If the vendor does not do the work, you will not receive consistent results. Achieving rankings today takes more than simply focusing on search engines. Ask the vendor and its clients if the SEO firm provides advice and set-up assistance for social networking sites such as Facebook, Google+, LinkedIn, and Twitter. Ask if they provide press release services. Ask if they can write articles for you. It takes a team of individuals to accomplish all of these items.

• **Ask about exclusivity.** Ask if your vendor offers exclusive representation for your city or town, or restricts the number of law firms it accepts in a given area. This is important for several reasons. You want them to help you grow, not sell you and then chase the next sale, which may be your competitor down the street or the highest bidder in your city. The vendor must have incentive to treat you like a partner and to help you grow. Also, you want to be able to share your ideas and not worry about your good ideas going down the street. You may wish to pay for an exclusivity option, if the vendor offers one.

• **Ask about tailor-made projects.** Ask the vendor's clients if the vendor analyzed their needs and goals, or if it simply applied its standard processes. Some SEO companies try to box their clients into their pre-packaged approach rather than tailor a campaign to fit the client.

• **Ask about PPC campaigns.** Ask if the vendor also provides complementary pay-per-click management. A well-developed organic SEO campaign, combined with a strategic pay-per-click campaign, can work well and be cost-effective.

- **Ask about site analytics.** Ask the vendor's references if the vendor provides personal one-on-one reviews of the firm's rankings and analytics on a regular basis. The statistics can include Google Analytics, server reports, ranking reports, general status reports and others. Ask if the company alerts the firm to shifts in the search engines and technology field, and offers specific recommendations for improving the website's performance.

Pay-Per-Click Campaigns

Another way to receive online exposure for your law firm is to use pay-per-click (PPC) ads. You can sign up for a Google PPC ad campaign by going to Google.com and selecting "Advertising." You can obtain a login and input your campaigns, the phrases you wish to target, the locale you wish to target, and the budget you wish to work.

One advantage of PPC ads over organic rankings is that your firm can quickly appear on Google's first search page for a targeted phrase. Organic rankings, on the other hand, may take weeks or months to accomplish this ranking. The best strategy is to rank for both.

You can manage the PPC campaign yourself or hire a consultant to help you. Consultants typically charge 10% - 20% of the expenditure for their time. Competent consultants can pay for themselves by helping you with your PPC descriptions, monitoring, budgets, competition comparison, geographic targeting and reporting. You can log in and view your ads. Effective descriptions and geographic targeting will bring you more clients for less money.

A Compelling Web Presence

It's crucial to bring visitors to your site, but the goal is turn them into clients. Your site should compel visitors to contact you – and make it easy for them to do so. Here's how:

Practical Advice. Proven Solutions.
www.PILMMA.org

- Place prominent contact forms at the top of the page.

- Make sure that your phone number is visible.

- Add features such as "Click to Call" or "Live Chat". *Click to Call* is a feature that allows a visitor to click on the Click to Call button and initiate a call to you. Before initiating the call, the visitor is asked to type in their name, email address, and phone number. That data is captured for you. Once they click on the Call-Me-Now button, the system calls the visitor's phone number and your phone number then connects you. If you are not available, the system takes a message. In either case, you have captured the visitor's contact information.

Live Chat is a feature embedded into your website and mobile platforms that allows you to communicate with the visitors to your website in real time. It works just as if the site visitor was calling into your office and speaking with a live operator on the phone except that it's online. You're able to ask visitors, "How can I help?" instantly without having to depend on them to call into your firm.

- Place a "Do I Have A Case?" or "Do I Need a Lawyer?" button on your website that scrolls downward and upward as the client scrolls down and up the page.

- If Verdicts and Settlements are permitted on websites in your state, it is good to link to your verdicts and settlements.

- Include a video center on your site. It is best to communicate with people in the way THEY are most comfortable.

- Content is still king, and many law firm sites now have hundreds of pages; some have a few thousand. Search engines and visitors like sites that provide a lot of information. You can keep your site clean and concise while still having a lot of content by having "Click here for more" hyperlinks at the bottom of pages. If you do not have time to develop your own content or blog, hire a vendor to help you.

• Mobile Marketing is a new method of reaching your potential prospects. More people perform Google searches on their iPhones and Androids than on a laptop or desktop. Google will actually penalize your website if it is not responsive. By responsive I mean it must adjust so it can easily be navigated on an iPad or mobile phone. It's not that your website should be responsive – it MUST be responsive.

Internet is so vital to a law firm's success these days that I felt I had to add an additional chapter from my trusted Internet advisor, Dale Tincher from Consultwebs.com. In the chapter, *Law Firm Marketing in a Virtual World*, Dale will detail what it really takes for a law firm to stand out and be successful in today's online marketing landscape.

While Dale will address website layout and organization, converting visitors to leads and how to truly solidify your rankings in searches, one topic that will be addressed by another expert is online video.

A Word About Online Video

YouTube, created in 2007, surpassed 100 million U.S. viewers in January 2009. To date, more than one billion unique users visit YouTube each month. According to Nielson, YouTube reaches more US adults ages 18-34 than any cable network. Videos are available on virtually every topic – and thousands of law firm videos have been uploaded. Millions of subscriptions happen each day. The number of people subscribing daily is up more than 3x since last year.

A video can have substantial impact on your website. No other medium has the effectiveness or persuasive power of video. Video content reaches potential clients – and keeps them on your website – in a way that a static page cannot. Online videos have been shown to hold an audience longer than simple text-based web pages, and they create greater product recall.

Practical Advice. Proven Solutions.
www.PILMMA.org

Video is so important, I asked Gerry Oginski, the guru for using online videos to market your law firm, to write a chapter for this new edition of my book. I know you will find it most informative.

CHAPTER 8:

Law Firm Marketing in a Virtual World

By Dale Tincher

Practical Advice. Proven Solutions.
www.PILMMA.org

If you could create the ultimate experience for a high value prospective client who walks into your office for the first time, how would you want that visit to play out?

Keep in mind that before coming into your office, the prospect visited your biggest competitor and, when she leaves your office, plans to visit another.

Who in your office would you want to greet her?

How would you want her to feel?

What would you tell her?

Would her experience be uniquely different from the one offered by your competition?

Answers to these questions are important because the initial impressions formed during that first visit are the most significant influencing factors to growing your practice. The majority of people buy and make decisions based on emotion. They hire you based on how you make them feel.

Imagine if the prospect were forming those first impressions before she even walked into your office.

Today, your website *is your virtual office.* The only difference is that your online presence offers potential clients the unique experience of walking into your office and considering your firm from home or on the go.

These individuals have the personal freedom to be invisible to you as they review your services. They are able to walk around your office at their leisure, pick up any book in your lobby and consider your wall art—all before speaking with you. Every prospective client who considers hiring your firm has the ability, thanks to the Internet, to review you, to rationalize a judgment and to decide consciously whether they want to hire you—all before picking up the phone or walking through your office

Practical Advice. Proven Solutions.
www.PILMMA.org

door. That takes the meaning of your website and overall Web reputation to a whole new level. Just like your office, your website is a place to sign new business.

Make It Easy For Them

The Internet offers people endless information and resources at their fingertips. Anyone with a smartphone has open access to obtain nearly any content imaginable instantly, and at their leisure. With the convenience and freedom of the ever-improving Web, along with the endless (and still growing!) options of available content, people are becoming more selective in where and how they spend their time on the Internet.

They are becoming more particular and choosy.

The bottom line: if your website does not quickly and conveniently provide users with what they are looking for, you will lose them. They know they have the option of hitting the "back" button and finding another relevant webpage.

Your website focus should be to provide a user-friendly layout with clear navigation and a wealth of helpful resources along with conversion channels that enable potential clients to contact your law firm when they decide they are ready.

Your website's success starts with the prioritization of your homepage. You need to arrange and organize your website's pages based on importance and relevancy. Rather than linking to all of your primary and sub-practice areas from your homepage, start planning by creating a pyramid chart, listing your most important pages at the top of the pyramid and filtering them down based on related subject matter and priority order. This will help you create a usable site structure for your website visitors.

Practical Advice. Proven Solutions.
www.PILMMA.org

Here is an example:

Homepage --- About Us --- Cases We Handle --- What Our Clients Say --- Contact

       | |

Attorney Bios   Practice Areas List

                 |

Related FAQs based on PA

Related Verdicts / Settlements based on PA

Your homepage should not make users feel overwhelmed. All too often, law firms have 20-plus options from which to choose on their homepage. A law firm has about six seconds to earn the user's attention and to assure him that he landed on the right Web page based on his search query.

Imagine needing to buy a television and walking into a store ready to make a purchase. As soon as you walk in, you see at least 100 televisions lining the walls. The TVs range from large to small, LCD to LED, Plasma to 4K. Assuming a sales representative does not approach you to offer assistance, you inevitably would begin to feel overwhelmed with the endless options. If you had not done your research prior to walking in the store, you would be lost. Options all too often create unnecessary clutter. They do not improve a user's experience, they ruin it. Today, less is more.

Once you have attracted a potential client to your website, you have to control the user experience by offering the user exactly what you want them to see. Group your pages by relevancy: If someone is interested in which practice areas your firm represents, he can find the answer easily by choosing "Cases We Handle." If he is more interested in reviewing your attorneys, he will click on "About Us." This layout requires more upfront strategic thought by you or your Web designer, but it will improve the user experience dramatically and result in more leads. In addition, it will retain visitors on your site longer, engage them and give you more opportunities to build customer confidence in your law firm.

The same concept applies when a prospective client walks into your physical office. If it is messy and cluttered, she will quickly make the assumption that you and your practice are disorganized. She will worry that your representation of her case will be similarly haphazard. Your online visitors make the same connection: If your website is clean and professional, they will, either intentionally or subconsciously, equate that to how you run your practice.

Google, following its Hummingbird search engine update (more to come on this algorithm update later in the chapter), has improved its search engine to deliver more precise results. Fewer users are directed to your homepage; instead, they now land directly on your site's more relevant inner pages. The same design mentality of "less is more" remains critical, requiring more work to plan the site structure.

If a visitor lands directly on your car accidents landing page, for example, you should provide her with links to all relevant pages within that practice area. If you have FAQs related to auto accidents or resources they can review—a downloadable article about "7 Things Most People Forget To Do After An Accident", relevant videos, testimonials and verdicts or settlements related to automobile injury cases you have handled—showcase them on this page! Naturally, visitors who land directly on your car accident page have an interest in seeing and reading all of those relevant pages.

By properly structuring your site, you are able to provide a phenomenal user experience and build confidence and trust. A well-conceived site ultimately will convert more visitors into paying clients. If you skip the step of prioritizing and structuring your pages, it will not matter how much traffic you drive to your website; you will never convert an optimal number of leads.

Practical Advice. Proven Solutions.
www.PILMMA.org

In Youtility: *Why Smart Marketing is about Help not Hype*, Jay Baer recommends creating internal systems to learn more about your client's needs and decision-making cycle. You will then be able to use this information to drive content and strategy.

Converting Visitors to Leads

Prospective clients will contact your law firm in one of three ways. They can: 1) fill out an inquiry through your contact form; 2) submit their information via live chat; or 3) call your office directly. The majority of visitors will call you. The second most important conversion channel is live chat. If you are not currently using all three methods on your site, you are losing leads.

While you absolutely want to have those three conversion methods on your site, there are additional ways you can encourage more conversions. From the moment prospects first land on your site, you have to ensure they are receiving a memorable experience with your law firm. Remember, people make decisions based on emotion. Custom photography and videos are key ways to personalize your site and separate your law firm from the competitor next door. Who in your office greets walk-in clients? Make sure your website visitors receive greetings from the same person(s) via photography or video.

Testimonials, reviews and past verdicts or settlements also dramatically increase leads. In a survey by Dimensional Research, 90% of the respondents claimed that their buying decision was influenced by positive online reviews. Nine out of 10 prospective clients are likely to read reviews of your law firm before calling you. If you are still neglecting the importance of reviews, this is your wake-up call.

Ken Hardison says that "a testimonial from a past client may be the most credible recommendation a prospect can get." He also advises, "What you say about yourself is good. What others say is *gold*."

Practical Advice. Proven Solutions.
www.PILMMA.org

Whether you are collecting the testimonials and reviews yourself and placing them on your site, or your former clients are going directly to Google+, Yelp and Avvo to post them, you will find that these will be some of the most critical marketing efforts to earn new business. Do not underestimate the power and influence of a positive online review.

Your Website Is Worthless... Unless!

Your site is of absolutely no value unless visitors are finding it. You may have the best design in town, but if your prospective clients are not able to find you, they are not able to consider you. That is why investing in online visibility is critical to staying ahead in the law firm marketing virtual world.

People are using the Web in a number of different ways. To establish a dominant online presence, you have to "fish where the fish are."

Your prospective clients are:

1. Searching Google with direct intent to hire a lawyer (e.g., "Chicago car accident attorney")

2. Researching in Google about their situation (e.g., "Options for families struggling to pay medical expenses after a car accident")

3. Spending time on Facebook, Twitter, Tumblr and Google+

4. Reading news on local and national news media sites (ESPN, CNN, FOX News, MarketWatch, hometown newspaper websites.)

5. Watching videos (YouTube, Vimeo)

6. Surfing the Web

7. Listening to on-demand music

Your prospective clients are spending more time online every year, whether on traditional desktop and laptop computers or on tablets, smartphones and other new devices. Your firm, therefore, has numerous opportunities to get in front of these prospects.

The marketing budget you allocate to the Web will dictate where you need to invest. The larger your budget, the wider the net you can cast. The best return on investment occurs through inbound marketing (as opposed to outbound marketing), which is the practice of delivering your message through useful content or engaging dialogue. Outbound marketing is more traditional advertising like billboards, TV and radio spots and Yellow Pages.

With outbound marketing, you pay to broadcast your message to a large audience with the understanding that only a small percentage will be interested and ready to convert.

Inbound marketing is generally less expensive and more targeted. It requires less of a "hard sell" and immediate call-to-action and instead focuses on engagement and interaction.

The Internet provides unlimited options to consumers, and those options make strategic inbound marketing one of the most effective marketing strategies ever devised. People tend to tune out advertising if it is not relevant to their real-time interests. The Web creates somewhat of an equalizing platform for large and small budget law firms.

Thought and strategy are more important than dumping dollars into a campaign (although "thought and strategy" often do require significant resources if done properly). The most successful law firms marketing online are those that have invested in helping and engaging prospective clients versus focusing primarily on persuading them to CALL NOW! No one likes to be sold. The minute a prospective client feels as though you are trying to sell them, they are turned off.

A successful inbound marketing strategy is one that educates, provides helpful resources and compels people to call you because of your expertise. Said differently, do not tell people how great you are; show them. Let them come to that conclusion themselves. When you master this approach, prospective clients will beat a path to your doorway.

Compelling content is one of the key ways to attract prospective clients. We all know we need to produce quality content, but actually doing it is much more difficult.

Content can take any number of forms. It may be static content, which is primarily used on your website as your core content pages: practice area pages, frequently asked questions, pages explaining relevant studies and other evergreen pages (those that remain relevant for a long period of time).

Blogs are another form of content. These article-type pages are typically more short-term relevant content and often less substantive than a core page of content. They are also generally tightly focused on a particular topic.

CLICK HERE to Request Your Free Guide on one of the following topics:
- Auto Accident
- Social Security Disability
- Workers' Compensation
- Auto Insurance
- Motorcycle Safety & Insurance

GET YOUR FREE GUIDE

Other content assets include downloadable "freebies." North Carolina injury law firm Hardison & Cochran has mastered this practice on its website, LawyerNC.com. This strategy allows you to collect contact information or connections on social media and stay in front of visitors (via targeted drip e-mail marketing campaigns and social media). Providing helpful resources around a visitor's area of need also helps you to establish your firm as an expert.

Each piece of content you create for your site should focus on the prospective client. Imagine you are in the market for a new vehicle and, in your research, you discover a local car dealership offering a free online "Guide to Buying a New Vehicle." After downloading the report, you learned interesting facts and helpful tips to consider with new vehicles (e.g., fuel efficiency comparisons or hands-free technology availability), questions to ask a dealership about lifetime benefits and warranties, pitfalls to avoid when financing through a dealership and many other resources that you never would have considered. The report was branded with that dealership's name, but there was never an uncomfortable sales pitch throughout the report. It was all about educating you and providing true value. What would your opinion be of that dealership? Would you consider visiting them and seeing what they had to offer?

Your firm should implement the same approach. Hiring a law firm can be an intimidating process. Offering helpful guides will attract prospective clients who are not yet in the hiring stage of the process. Without the downloadable guide, you likely would have lost them, never to return.

Hitting a Content Schedule

The practice of blogging just to be blogging is dead (or should be). If you are not providing value, you are wasting your time. The question should not be "how many posts should I write this week?" but rather, "what are my clients' needs and concerns and how can I address them?" You will see better results putting together one substantive, valuable blog article than spending time writing five articles that go unread and unshared. The ultimate focus of every article should be the prospective client.

The same goes for static, core content. Just because your competitor has 300 pages doesn't mean you need that many to be competitive. Google's algorithm no longer focuses primarily on quantity. The metrics considered when analyzing your site now primarily consider qualitative measures. For example, how long do visitors stay on your workers' compensation page after landing on it? How many visitors click into deeper, relevant pages once they hit your burn injuries page? Are they sharing your page on their social media channels? Are they downloading reports? Are they commenting and interacting on your blog?

If the metrics indicate strong activity on your site, it is clear that people are enjoying your website and content, and thus, it is likely a strong result for future searchers with similar search queries. That is what Google is acknowledging in a quality website today.

Pandas, Penguins and Hummingbirds, OH MY!

Google makes frequent changes to its search algorithm, as well as to how it displays search results. The changes will continue. It is inevitable. The search company has suggested that it implements roughly 600 changes to the algorithm each year—most of which are minor. Google's primary goal with search is to provide the most useful, relevant results so that users will continue to come back and feel confident that Google will provide them with exactly the right content each time. To accomplish that, Google closely follows search trends and adapts based on the end user's preferences. Visit moz.com/google-algorithm-change for the latest algorithm updates.

The most notable recent change to Google's search engine was the Hummingbird update in late August 2013. The goal of this overhaul was to return better, more precise search results. As users became more detailed in their search queries, expecting specific information, Google adjusted to deliver precise results to match the users' search expectations. Hummingbird was much different than the prior search engine updates referred to as Panda and Penguin. It was an actual overhaul of the search engine that replaced the old engine with a new one. Panda and Penguin were algorithmic updates, focused primarily on penalizing sites whose rankings were achieved with poor or unnatural content and backlinks, respectively.

With Hummingbird, Google is delivering a more precise search to improve the user experience for the searcher, often delivering users to inner pages rather than a site's homepage. This eliminates the unnecessary steps of a user having to guide himself through your site to find the content he is looking for. With this update, websites that have deep, substantive and useful content were rewarded with broader search engine visibility.

It is impossible to accurately anticipate future algorithm shifts. Law firms should worry less about algorithms and focus their time on creating content that is useful to prospective clients. Traditional search engine optimization (SEO) is still important, but the best investment of your resources is to focus efforts on creating websites and content with value and substance. Fundamental strategies that will benefit a law firm's Web presence for the long term are Google algorithm-proof.

Visit **goo.gl/YxdJb** for Search Engine Land's 10 Fundamental Tips to Improve Your SEO.

Planning a Successful Future on the Web

Law firms that connect organic search, social media and mobile marketing with their community and content will thrive on the Web. Firms that expect to pay an SEO vendor to "take the ball and run with it" will not experience optimal results. The reason is simple: The Internet is becoming more personalized. Fundamental SEO will carry a business only so far. Your firm has to take the next step and tie all of the channels together. This is accomplished through a cohesive offline and online marketing strategy.

Google is evolving to be much more than just a search engine. The search engine giant wants to understand its users and it has full access to data that makes this goal possible through Gmail, social media profiles, calendars, search history and behavior, location and interests. Google's analysts have a wealth of users' personal information at their fingertips and they are using it to get even better at delivering the right information at the right time (with the goal of delivering information before users even know they need it).

Today's search engine also is getting better at recognizing voice and natural language search. Imagine artificial intelligence technology that understands you on a personal level and delivers unique, useful information based on you and your preferences. Sounds like the ideal personal assistant, right? That is Google's vision for search. Affiliate marketing veteran Rae Hoffman puts the search engine giant's motivations into perspective. "Google doesn't want to make websites popular, they want to rank popular websites," she says. "If you don't understand the difference, you're in for one hell of an uphill climb"

To achieve and maintain a dominant presence on the Web, your law firm has to embrace and prepare for that evolution of consumer information gathering and consumption.

To do this, you must learn to see social media as a necessity. It is not enough just to be there. You have to utilize a strategy that builds your network and engages your community. Very few people will organically "like" or follow a law firm business. You have to give them a reason to connect with you. You have to get involved in the community and support charities and causes within your local areas.

If you are a personal injury attorney, you have limitless opportunities to relate causes or charities to your practice. Distracted driving, drunk driving, product safety, water or boating safety, consumer safety and bicycle safety/helmet awareness are only a few examples of how you can establish an advocacy campaign for the betterment of your community—all the while building a strong brand for your firm. From there, you can leverage that advocacy campaign through scholarships, giveaways and local events.

Partnering with organizations or charities with related interests gives you an opportunity to leverage online relationships, which

Practical Advice. Proven Solutions.
www.PILMMA.org

almost always result in quality and natural backlinks for your site. (Note that backlinks are a current positive signal for SEO, but likely will fade as Google becomes more focused on personalized search results and uses more of a qualitative metric algorithm.) The larger network you build online, the more opportunity you will have to attract website visitors when they are in need of resources on your site or have an immediate interest in hiring a law firm.

Your firm also should be prepared to consider the growing opportunities for strategic paid advertising online. Highly targeted Pay Per Click (PPC) campaigns will become an increasingly useful tool as Google improves personalized search results. Google will continue to reward searches that increase its ad revenue and your firm can take advantage of this practice to diversify your website traffic and leads. But paid search is not a tactic that your firm should wait to implement. Current opportunities for PPC campaigns are worthwhile and a Google Analytics Certified Partner and landing page conversion specialist will be able to realize value on your PPC investment.

When first starting a marketing push, many firms have made a common error: identifying Web advertising as "earned" and, therefore, failing to budget for a proper paid search campaign. While SEO is vital, seasoned marketers know that PPC is also critical. PPC beats other marketing efforts—including television advertisements—by cost-per-lead (CPL). After all, if online paid search results in an $800 cost per case and TV ads require a $1,000-per-case investment, then PPC is the clear winner.

To remain successful on the Web, you will need a creative marketing strategy. The Internet is more dynamic than ever and requires dedicated resources to plan, organize and implement successful campaigns. Firms that see the potential and act accordingly will experience tremendous results and significant ROI. There are no shortcuts to the future of legal Web marketing

Practical Advice. Proven Solutions.
www.PILMMA.org

in this virtual world. Build relationships with influencers and community and industry leaders. Create stellar content through static and blog pages, video and downloadable assets. Grow your social networks, especially Google+. And commit to offering that ultimate experience and first impression for your prospective clients.

Practical Advice. Proven Solutions.
www.PILMMA.org

CHAPTER 9:

Video Marketing in the Age of YouTube
By Gerry Oginski, Esq.

By now, you realize that traditional forms of marketing your law practice are no longer as relevant as they used to be. Who still uses the Yellow Pages anymore? Instead, many of us go online to search for information.

Searching For Information

Think about how a viewer searches for information. They have a particular legal problem. They want to learn more about their problem or about their injuries. They go on to Google or some other search engine and type in their problem. Now they are in search and find mode looking for answers to their legal problem.

Consumers want to know how things work. They want to know how the legal process works. They want to learn more about understanding their injuries. They want to learn from people who have gone through very same problem.

If they are searching for an attorney to help them solve their problem, they want to see that an attorney has significant experience handling their particular matter.

Importantly, a consumer will be totally turned off if you turn your marketing messages into a pitch fest that basically screams "Come to me because I'm great! I've been doing this 25 years and I have experience handling the types of cases you have."

A better approach in today's day of the Internet and YouTube is to provide them with an education-based message that teaches and educates them.

By teaching and educating your ideal client or consumer who is actively searching for you and your legal services, you become the "go-to" expert.

Practical Advice. Proven Solutions.
www.PILMMA.org

When a consumer does a search on Google and the results show 10 websites, the consumer begins to compare and contrast the information they find in each and every website. The majority of attorneys today are not making good use of one of the best media sources available, video.

Many attorneys are still in the Stone Age and refuse to use any "new media" that they are not comfortable with and have not used in the past. There are others, who we call "old-school" who still think marketing is beneath them and they refuse to do any active marketing. That's actually a great thing for you and me, why? It allows us the opportunity to attract more ideal clients to us.

What Video Can Do For You

The remarkable thing about using video is that it allows a viewer to see us, hear us and begin to trust us before they ever walk into our office. It allows us to pre-position our services as the go-to expert having the knowledge, experience and expertise they are looking for, without us ever having to say "Come to me because I'm an expert."

As you likely know by now, Google is the biggest search engine in the world. I'm assuming that you have a website and have devoted significant resources to maintain your website and do everything possible to optimize it so that it gets high rankings in the search engines.

In all likelihood you update your website on a frequent basis since the search engines love fresh new relevant content. If you are like me, you'll add blog posts, articles, frequently asked questions and other useful content on a frequent basis. You know that doing so makes your website more visible and more likely that a consumer who is searching for your information will find your great content.

Practical Advice. Proven Solutions.
www.PILMMA.org

YouTube Is A Search Engine

Do you know what the 2nd largest search engine in the world is, directly behind Google?

The answer is YouTube.

Do you know who owns YouTube?

The answer is Google. There's a direct correlation and interconnectivity between the two.

Lawyers who fail to use video to market their practices today are invisible to the second largest search engine in the world.

Think about that.

If you do not have great educational video to market your practice today, you are invisible to the second largest search engine in the world. Why would anyone intentionally ever do that?

Why invest so many resources to make yourself visible on the largest search engine in the world, but ignore the fact that they are invisible to the second largest search engine. That makes absolutely no sense.

If you have made the decision to invest in yourself and your law firm and learn how to market yourself effectively, one of the best investments you can make is to create attorney videos.

Here's why.

Video is the best way to communicate with a potential new client and consumer short of them meeting you face to face in your office. Video allows you to create an entire marketing system that consistently allows viewers to find you, learn from you and contact you for more information. We as a society are becoming more dependent on the Internet for our information. Your goal as an attorney who is seeking to market your practice is to create a way for your consumers to learn about what you do, to see how confident you are, to see how knowledgeable you are all without ever leaving their home or their mobile device.

A consumer who is searching for an attorney online does not know a lawyer nor do they know someone who can refer them to an attorney. As a result, they are trying to learn as much as possible about whether they can trust you.

Building Trust With Your Viewer

It is extremely difficult to build up trust from an article or blog post. It can be done, but when you compare the different media that generates trust the quickest way possible, you will see that video is the ideal way to do that. Since we live in an un-trusting world, and lawyers, by history, do not have a stellar reputation, video allows us the ability to build trust with our viewer, show them our competence and make them feel warm and invited when we ask them to call for more information.

Video Marketing Works

As someone who personally uses great educational video every day to market my solo practice in one of the most competitive markets in the country, I can tell you that video marketing works.

I receive calls and e-mails every single day from potential clients who always start out the same way "Mr. Oginski, I just watched your video about this topic...can I ask you some questions?"

Currently, I have over 750 videos to market my solo practice and the people who contact me to see if I can help them say the same thing over and over again. "Your videos are so informative and educational. Nobody else provides this type of information."

What To Talk About In An Attorney Video

Remarkably, I don't provide any legal advice in my videos. Nor do I ever talk about myself.

Every attorney I talk to asks me the same question...

"If I can't talk about myself or my law firm, and I cannot give legal advice, what the heck can I talk about?"

The answer will shock you. The answer will be eye-opening.

There is a lot for you to talk about. You have a tremendous fund of knowledge about your legal specialty. You can explain to your viewers how the legal process works. You can explain in a video what you look for in order to evaluate whether someone has a valid case. Remember, your ideal consumer or client likely has never been through the legal process before.

They likely do not know the steps involved in the initial meeting all the way through to its conclusion. You on the other hand, deal with this every day and assume that everybody has this knowledge. The reality is that they do not.

You can use video to engage your viewers by showing them how the cases you handle work. You can use video to describe certain types of injuries which will showcase your knowledge and expertise. You can use video to explain the case that you handled and how you were able to help a particular client.

Doing this on video gives you an opportunity to teach and educate your ideal clients and consumers about matters that are directly related to them. You never ever have to say "I care," or "I give personal attention." Those clichéd phrases will do nothing to attract your viewer to you.

Practical Advice. Proven Solutions.
www.PILMMA.org

TV Ads Are So Different From Online Video

If you have done any type of television advertising for your law firm, I will tell you right now that creating video to market your practice online is totally different. The strategies you use to create TV ads are totally inapplicable to creating great educational online video.

TV ads are usually 30 second spots screaming the same thing. "Injured? In an accident? If so, call me. I've been doing this type of work for 20 years..."

Online video marketing messages are 2-3 minutes long and give you the opportunity to explain to your viewer what they need to know.

Let me give you an example.

Interruption Based Marketing

TV lawyer ads are based upon something known as interruption-based marketing. This means that while you are pleasantly watching your show a commercial comes on and jolts you into believing you must take immediate action right now. You were not thinking about your legal matter. You were not contemplating hiring an attorney. You are just in the middle of enjoying your show. Now this loud and sometimes obnoxious commercial comes on interrupting your thoughts and your patterns.

Don't get me wrong, TV advertising can be remarkably successful if done in a targeted campaign that is consistent. That requires a significant marketing budget. However, once you turn off that marketing budget, your ads no longer run. Your ideal consumers who are watching TV will never see you again once you turn off that spigot.

Practical Advice. Proven Solutions.
www.PILMMA.org

Video Provides A Great Return On Your Investment

In contrast, when you create educational online video, after your initial production costs, there are no other additional expenses to maintain those videos online. That means that they run 24 hours a day, 365 days a year, forever. There is no other marketing media available today that has such a low price point entry.

Those videos work for you night and day, when you're at work, when you're sleeping, when you were on vacation and literally all the time.

The reason why online video works so well is because it allows a consumer who is actively searching for information to find your great content, consume your content and then follow your call to action. You are not interrupting anyone's TV show by creating great online attorney video. You are creating a perfect message that is simply waiting for your ideal client.

Why Would I Create A Video With This Title: "What Is Testicular Torsion?"

Do you know why a solo medical malpractice attorney in New York would create a video titled "What is Testicular Torsion?"

It sounds really odd for a lawyer to be talking about such a painful condition, but think about who might want information about such a video.

A man who believes his testicular torsion was not timely diagnosed and lost a testicle would likely be the ideal person to search for and watch this video. A parent whose child has just been diagnosed with this condition and has lost his testicle may also be the ideal person to watch this video.

So let's go back and answer the original question. Why would I ever create a video with this title as the video topic?

The answer is simple.

I wanted to attract a targeted and specific client who had this particular problem. You see, I had recently handled a case involving a young child who, because of an undiagnosed and untreated testicular torsion, lost his testicle. I wanted to handle more of those cases.

I knew that parents of such a child and adults who have this condition may want more information about how this condition is diagnosed and treated. My video simply educated them about what the condition was, how doctors diagnosed it and commonly accepted treatments for this problem.

Viewer Comments

Since YouTube is also a social network, much like Facebook, Twitter and LinkedIn, you would be shocked to read the comments that appear underneath this testicular torsion video. I say shocked because people are actually asking me for medical advice about what to do with groin pain, believing that they may have testicular torsion.

Now ask yourself this question:

Why would someone with a possible testicular torsion ask a medical malpractice lawyer for medical advice?

"I'm Not A Doctor, Dammit!"

Don't they know that I am only an attorney who handles these cases and not a physician? Don't they have common sense that if they have a medical problem they should go to the hospital or to their doctor?

Practical Advice. Proven Solutions.
www.PILMMA.org

More importantly, what could I have possibly said in my video that would make these people believe I have information about this particular condition that they are now reaching out to me for medical advice?

There is an important teaching point here. As I mentioned before, I do not give legal advice in my videos. Nor do I talk about myself.

What I Did To Generate Lots Of Comments

In this particular video I simply described the medical condition. I explained what symptoms a man or child would have when they have this excruciatingly painful problem. I explained what the literature shows about having a limited window of opportunity to diagnose and treat this condition before the blood supply gets cut off requiring the surgical removal of the dead testicle.

I did nothing more than showcase my knowledge and expertise on this particular condition.

For those of you curious to know, in every one of the comments posted on YouTube from people asking me for medical advice, I immediately notified them that I could not answer their questions since I am only an attorney who handles these medical malpractice matters here in New York. They must go to their emergency room immediately or to their doctor to get answers to their medical questions.

How You Can Use This Strategy In Your Own Practice

Think about the different ways you can use this technique in your own marketing. The answers are abundant and will allow you to create fantastic types of educational content to showcase your knowledge and expertise.

Practical Advice. Proven Solutions.
www.PILMMA.org

I Challenge You...

When you create your attorney videos, I have a challenge for you that I would like you to accept. I challenge you to remove these words in your videos:

"I,"
"Me,"
"We,"
"Our,"
"My law firm,"
"Our law firm,"

I guarantee that by removing these words from your attorney videos you will change the focus of your video from being lawyer-centric and instead focus on your ideal clients and consumers.

The best way I can explain it is that you will change the focus from "Me, me, me" to "You, you, you".

Doing this will revolutionize your marketing messages, not just in your videos but every marketing message you use today and in the future. Guaranteed.

YouTube Is A Social Network

Not only is YouTube the second largest search engine in the world, but it is also a social network. Most lawyers and attorneys who use YouTube to market their services forget this fact.

Lawyers who take advantage of this social interactivity see much more benefit when using video compared the lawyers who simply upload and forget about their videos.

Your goal when creating a video message on YouTube is to get a viewer to call and contact your office. **That is your single and only goal.**

Practical Advice. Proven Solutions.
www.PILMMA.org

Your goal is not to create a brand. Your goal is not to create a public service message. Your goal is to teach and educate your consumers in order for them to recognize you as an expert and that you are the only solution to their problem.

Your Only Goal When Creating Video

Your goal is to convert an online viewer into a caller. If your videos fail to do this, then there is a problem with either planning, production, publishing, optimizing, your call to action, lack of social interaction, or even promotion of your video.

Lawyers who simply upload video to YouTube and do nothing else are using the "Hope" method of marketing. That's a method where you throw out a marketing message and hope somebody will find it. You hope it will be your ideal client. You hope the message will be compelling. You hope the message will engage them so they will want more information. You hope they will call you based upon your message and your good looks.

I will tell you right now that the hope of method of marketing simply does not work.

Strategies You Can Implement Right Now...

Here's what you need to do to create compelling video that will convert a viewer into a caller:

1. Create a compelling headline.

2. Present your material in an engaging and interesting manner. If you are a typically boring attorney and present your material in a monotone voice I will guarantee that no one will watch your video.

3. Create an interesting description complete with all of your contact information.

Practical Advice. Proven Solutions.
www.PILMMA.org

4. Talk about something important that your viewer (ideal client) wants or needs to know.

5. Always give a call to action at the end of your video telling your viewers what to do next.

6. Give your viewers multiple ways to contact you. They don't only want to call you. They may want to e-mail you. They may want to reach out on Facebook. They may want to talk to you on Twitter. By only allowing them to reach out to you with one method, you are limiting the way your ideal clients reach you.

A few YouTube strategies that will help you immediately

1. Make your headline interesting. If you want to learn how to model great headlines, I encourage you to read the New York Post for its headlines.

2. Create a word-for-word transcript of your video and then insert it into YouTube. This will help the search engines understand what you're talking about.

3. Create spotlight annotations. At the end of every YouTube video, you are presented with a grid of six, nine or even 12 other "related" videos. This means that any viewer can now go elsewhere and watch other similar videos. By creating spotlight annotations, you can give your viewers the opportunity to instead watch more of your own YouTube videos rather than a competitor's videos or something totally unrelated.

4. You need to create a supplemental blog post for every single video you create. Remember, your online website is the center of your online universe. Think of it as being the hub of the spokes of a wheel. The spokes are content leading into and out of your website. Your goal is to drive traffic into and out of your website for viewers to see your content from multiple sources.

5. You need to create a frequently asked questions list for every video.

6. You need to create an extended article for every video you create.

7. The reason this is so important is that viewers find your material in different ways. Two thirds of all adults who go online prefer to watch video compared to read text. That's a fact according to Pew research. In addition, the search engines love text as well as video.

You need to create fresh new relevant video content on a consistent and frequent basis.

The search engines will reward you over time if you consistently do this. In addition, by creating fresh new relevant video content you literally push out your competition because I guarantee they will not be creating video content as often and as consistently as you do.

Also, if you create video I strongly urge you not to put it all up on one day. There is an important strategic reason for this. Remember what I said earlier that the search engines reward you for creating fresh new relevant content?

If you were to dump out 30 new videos all on one day, the search engines would be happy you put up all that great content. However, when you fail to put up any more content on day two or three or the next week or month, you've lost the benefit of putting up fresh new relevant content that the search engines actively want and look for.

YouTube specifically encourages people to upload video on a consistently fresh new basis. When you have great content, simply drip it out over time and you achieve a much greater benefit than putting it all up online at once.

Practical Advice. Proven Solutions.
www.PILMMA.org

A Video Guru Gets It Wrong

I was at a legal marketing seminar recently when a video production 'expert' was talking about video and was asked whether it's okay to put up all the video they shot in one day. The presenter gleefully agreed that it did not matter and strongly recommended putting the attorney videos up all in one day.

After the presentation was over, six lawyers approached me and asked whether this strategy was correct. The answer is "No." It goes against YouTube's own teachings and directives. Putting up fresh new relevant content on a consistent basis always trumps putting out a lot of content on just one day.

Another Video Guru Gets It Wrong

Let me share with you another quick story involving another legal seminar I was at for chief marketing officers of some very large law firms in New York City. I was a panelist with 3 other marketing and video people. There was a video "expert" on the panel who had done a lot of work for these large corporate law firms. She clearly had a lot of experience creating corporate style videos. She was asked whether there was any way to link your YouTube video directly to your website in the form of a clickable link on the video. She said "No."

She was wrong.

Another panelist and I had to correct her.

If you are a YouTube partner, you can now create a clickable link on your video that will allow a viewer to click directly from your video to your website.

She obviously didn't know this. But she came across authoritatively with her immediate answer that this was not possible.

Practical Advice. Proven Solutions.
www.PILMMA.org

What she didn't know was that this is an important strategy to use and one that was never available before. Why not? YouTube never wanted you to leave the YouTube world by clicking to an outside URL.

Now you can do it but it comes with a caveat. YouTube says that if you do this you will lose the benefit of having the viewer watch your video in total which means you will not register the total number of views and it may affect your search engine rankings over time. A double-edged sword.

Does Video Marketing Work?

Judge for yourself...

$5.1 Million dollar settlement in a case involving a brain injured infant at birth

$1 million settlement, failure to diagnose brain tumor

$840,000 wrongful death, failure to diagnose sepsis following elective hernia surgery

$300,000 fall from bed, subdural hematoma, death three weeks later

$495,000 wrongful death following bunion surgery nine months later

$395,000 wrongful death, failure to diagnose sepsis following GYN surgery

These are just a handful of cases I've taken in and successfully resolved as a direct result of potential new clients watching my videos and then picking up the phone to say "Mr. Oginski, I just saw your video about this topic, can I ask you some questions?"

Just Uploading To YouTube Is Not Enough

If you think you can create some video and simply post to YouTube and just leave it there and do nothing else, I will tell you right now that you have only one part of a three-legged stool. That stool would topple over.

Creating video to market your practice is a wonderful system that can drive traffic to you and your website and make you well known in your community as the go-to expert. However, there's more to it than just uploading a video to YouTube.

Once you have created a video and uploaded it, you then have to optimize the video. You need to create a compelling headline. You need to create an interesting description with all of your contact information. You need to create keywords and tags so that the search engines will recognize what type of content you have.

You need to create a word-for-word transcript to use behind the scenes in YouTube. By the way, you should never put the transcript in the description box. The description is where you put a detailed summary of what you are talking about. Not a transcript.

You need to create a supplemental blog post that will go on your website. You also need to create an article about the topic that will also appear on your website or some other location online. You'll need to create a frequently asked questions list with answers on the same topic. What this does is give a viewer who is searching for this information multiple sources in which to find your great content. You never want to limit your content to just one place online.

That builds the second leg of the stool.

What is the third leg of this stool? It's promoting your video through social media. It's using Facebook, Twitter, LinkedIn, newsletters, and other media that you use to promote your great new videos.

You cannot keep your videos a secret and 'hope' they will be found. You have to promote them. You have an obligation.

Your obligation is to yourself, your family, and to your law firm. You must now tell the world about your great new video content.

How Not To Promote Your New Videos

When using social media to promote your videos do not simply say "Check it out. I created a new video you need to watch."

Why is that not acceptable? Because it does not give the reader or viewer the answer to the question "Why?"

Why should they watch your video? You have not given them a valid reason. That's why when using social media you must always, always give your viewer a valid reason about why they should be watching your great content.

Here's a hint... Always let them know this will educate them and teach them about a particular topic. This way there's less resistance, there is a curiosity factor and it will make them smarter by learning a new piece of information.

Hopefully you are now beginning to see the benefits of creating great attorney video that teaches and educates your ideal clients and consumers. You recognize how important it is to be able to convey your message in the form of a video that will allow a viewer to see you, hear you and begin to trust you before they ever come into your office to meet you.

Creating great video is a game changer for most attorneys. It literally can revolutionize the way you practice law and here's why.

Practical Advice. Proven Solutions.
www.PILMMA.org

Video Can Revolutionize Your Practice

When a new caller calls your office for information, you can create a series of videos that they can receive every day prior to them coming in for a scheduled conference. You can use it to indoctrinate your new client by teaching them things that they should know that they did not know before. You can explain how the legal process works. You can explain your office procedures. You can give them great information about their type of matter, before they ever walk in the door.

Doing this builds up trust. You're not selling anything. You're simply teaching and educating people about things that you know. By creating a video series like this you also eliminate the need to repeat these things on a daily basis to your new potential clients. By the time they come into your office and meet you, they will have learned a tremendous amount of information about how you help people with this type of problem.

This is an incredible psychological motivating factor when they finally do meet you. They feel as if they've known you for a long time. When they look around your office and realize it's the same setting where you were shooting your videos they feel comfortable. It's a familiar feeling. They feel like they have been there before.

There is nothing more remarkable than when a potential new client walks into your office, shakes your hand, smiles at you and says "I feel like I have been here before," or "I feel like I already know you." The only way that can happen is when you create video that educates and teaches your viewers.

How Can I Do This?

By now, you are beginning to realize the incredible benefits of creating great video. You should now be getting all excited about figuring out how to do this for your practice. The key question for you to answer at this point is how to get this done?

You know that really smart attorneys take action on great strategies and ideas. The super-smart attorneys are ones who act quickly to implement great ideas you just learned. But, before you run out and buy all your video equipment to start shooting video, let me ask you a series of questions...

Do you really want to be a video producer, a video editor and video publisher in addition to practicing law? You really want to go through the learning curve of understanding and learning how to create video from start to finish? If you do, I congratulate you. I would consider you to be a "Do-it-Yourselfer" like me.

Did you know that the majority of lawyers simply want nothing to do with marketing? They recognize it is a necessary evil and will do everything possible to hire the right people to get this done for them. If you are a little closer to the attorney who prefers to have this done for you, I congratulate you as well. You have taken the step of recognizing that you don't want to learn how to do all this and simply want someone with experience to do it for you. You simply have to figure out your next step to make this happen.

I always analogize this decision to the following story.

What's your choice?

Are you the type of person who likes to fix your car for two weeks after it breaks down on the highway and tow it to your home, put it up on blocks and work on it every day after work? Or are you the type of person who would rather just call the mechanic to tow your car to the garage and have it fixed the next day?

Maybe you like to tinker and when your watch breaks you spend 3 days looking for that tiny little screw that went into that microscopic hole that held the watch spring that just doesn't want to go back into place. Or maybe you're the type of person who takes their watch in to the jeweler and they'll fix it in one day without any hassle whatsoever.

Are you the type of person who climbs a 20 foot ladder in the pouring rain because of the hole in the roof, or are you the type of person who would rather call a construction guy to fix it?

Is your time worth more than the effort to do it yourself?

Or, would you rather pay someone to handle tasks that you simply don't want to do; have no desire to do; or have no intent to learn?

Let me share with you a fact that will help you understand and solidify whatever decision you choose. If you go out and create video on your own without learning all the details involved, there's a good chance that the technical quality of your video will be less than ideal. You might have a problem with the video. Your lighting may be off. The audio may stink. Your background or frame may not be pleasing.

There may be something distracting in your video. I've seen this thousands and thousands of times. Smart lawyers with really good intentions are trying to be a video producer, video editor and video publisher because someone told them that all they have to do is take out their iPhone and create quick & dirty video and publish it to YouTube and that will drive traffic to them and their website.

A Viewer Correlates Our Legal Ability With The Quality Of Our Video

The unfortunate reality is that our ideal clients and consumers who are searching for our information online to help solve their legal problems correlate our video ability with our legal ability. It's

Practical Advice. Proven Solutions.
www.PILMMA.org

true. It's not a fair assumption for them to make, but it's one they do every day.

There is a subconscious recognition that an attorney who creates crappy video means that their legal ability is on the same level. Besides when you put up video with technical distractions a viewer will not be forgiving since there are many other videos and attorneys to listen to. Viewers will not be very forgiving when watching a poorly done video. They will think that the attorney's legal abilities are just as affected as his ability to create a technically proficient video.

Keep that in mind when deciding whether to create video on your own or hire someone to do it for you.

I also caution you not to listen to video experts who tell you how easy it is to create video using your iPhone, tablet, iPad, your flip phone, Kodak Zi8, or some other device.

Creating video can be lots of fun...if you have the time, energy and desire to do this.

Take it from me, I have been told I was the very first attorney to create an education-based message using video back in 2006. At that time, I was just starting to learn about education-based marketing in the form of articles and blog posts.

I knew nothing about video at that time. I knew nothing about audio. I knew nothing about lighting. But I had this great idea when I saw a tiny new website come online called YouTube. They said they were accepting user generated video content.
The problem was I had no idea what that meant nor did anyone else.

As I explored this tiny little new website I began to see some enterprising TV production companies throw their attorney commercials onto this new website. I could not understand why anyone in their right mind would voluntarily want to watch 30 seconds of an attorney screaming "Come to me because I'm great. Come to me because I handle these cases. Call me now!"

The problem with these attorney commercials is that they never took the time to explain "Why?"

Why should I call you instead of the next attorney I see in the next few minutes? Why are you different? Why are you the right one for me? You haven't taught me anything in your 30 second TV pitch.

That's when I thought about using video as a tool to create an education-based message to people who were actively searching for me online.

I Knew Nothing About Creating Video

You should know that I didn't even have a video camera. I had a Mac computer with a tiny pinhole WebCam and did not even know how to turn it on. The sad reality was that I had to ask my kids how to turn on the video camera on my computer.

It took me weeks to try and figure out how to create video and from those frustrating efforts I finally figured out how to do it. My first video was 6 1/2 minutes long. It was the worst video I ever created in my life.

Sitting 7 inches away from the computer you could easily see the glare in my eyeglasses from the reflection of the computer screen. The video was dark. It was grainy. It was pixelated. I put up a video projector screen behind me so people couldn't see me sitting in my home office. I was wearing a shirt, tie and jacket and was wearing shorts while sitting at my computer. You could only see me from the waist up.

A remarkable thing happened after I finally figured out how to get this video up on YouTube. Over the next few weeks and months, I began to get calls from people who watched this video. The remarkable thing is that they said the same words every time they called...

"Mr. Oginski, I just saw your video about this topic, can I ask you some questions?"

My Family Thought I Was Nuts

You should know that in my desire to create this new form of education based video message my family was not supportive of me. They couldn't understand why I was spending hours, days, weeks and months sitting in my office frustrated and agonizing how to make this work. My wife was totally unsupportive. "I would never watch an attorney on video! Why are you wasting your time? Go do something productive like prep for your deposition tomorrow." Comforting words about reality.

Likewise, my kids had the same reaction. They would see me sitting on the computer for hours and hours on end becoming edgy, frustrated and pulling out whatever little hair I had left on my head. They would plead with me to come in and tell them a bedtime story since it was getting late. I promised to do it repeatedly, but before I knew it, hours went by and my kids went to bed.

They kept asking why I was wasting my time trying to create video for the Internet. They couldn't imagine anyone wanting to watch a lawyer talk about legal things online.

My Secretary Forwards My Calls

In 2006, when my secretary would leave for the day, she would forward all of my calls to my cell phone. I would be in the car with my family when a call came in, and always put it in on speaker.

Over the next few months, something remarkable began to happen.

Over and over again I began to get calls from people who saw my video calling to ask me questions. Not every caller had a valid case. In fact since I handle medical malpractice cases in New York, I am extremely selective about the cases I handle. I reject 99 out of 100 calls to my office...and that's just on the phone!

But here's the critical point. I was doing something that now was generating calls to my office. I never had such a system in place before. It was only through those phone calls that I would receive while I was in the presence of my family did they begin to realize that this video marketing actually works.
I will share with you another little secret. It has probably been the only time in my 25 years of marriage to my wife that she has turned to me and said "All right honey. I never should have doubted you. You were right." That's something I will always cherish. The fact that I was right and she was not :-).

What Are You Going To Do Now?

So the real question you have to consider at this point is, what are you going to do in order to create great attorney video to market your practice?

You can learn how to do all this on your own and if that's the mindset you have, then I encourage you to do so. You will find it very enjoyable if not frustrating and aggravating at times.

To Learn More...

If you'd like to learn more about creating video on your own I encourage you to explore the Lawyers Video Studio website (LawyersVideoStudio.com).

After doing this now for many years I realized that attorneys needed help because there was no one in the country teaching attorneys how to create video on their own. As a result, I actually created an online video tutorial program that teaches you and shows you step-by-step exactly how to create video from the inception of creating your ideas, creating your compelling content, teaching you what I do, showing you how to plan and produce your videos as well as shooting them, editing them, packaging them and publishing them online. Then I teach you step-by-step what you need to do once your videos are online working for you.

Sign Up For Video Marketing Tips & Strategies

In addition, if you want more great video marketing tips and strategies then I recommend you sign up for my RSS blog post feed on my website (LawyersVideoStudio.com). Great consistent content three times a week.

Learning how to create video marketing systems in my practice has been one of the most revolutionary and remarkable ways that changed how I practice law. It has allowed me the ability to create a lifestyle practice rather than become a slave to my law firm.

As always, the choice of what you want to do is always up to you.

So, are you a little closer to the attorney who wants to learn how to do it yourself or are you a little closer to the attorney who wants an experienced video marketing company to do it all for you? Whichever one you are closer to, my suggestion is to act on these great ideas and begin to implement immediately. That's what really smart attorneys do.

The longer you wait to create great educational video, the longer you will be invisible to the second largest search engine in the world. Keep that in mind.

CHAPTER 10:

Social Media

Throughout history, and today, this adage rings true: No matter how good something is, someone will find a way to make it better. The Internet is no exception. Around the turn of the century new phrases started emerging in Internet lingo, social media, and Web 2.0 (the terms are interchangeable). While you can find thousands of definitions in Google for these terms, they simply mean having a web presence that allows people to interact with you and your law firm.

The best thing about these tools is that most are free and very easy to use. You can also use them consistently to build your SEO organically.

Before we get into the world of social media, remember this: there is no exact formula for manipulating these tools to your advantage. Different people do it different ways. The best way to design your plan is to take time and see how others are using social media. Then decide what is best for you.

Social media is definitely the direction large entities -- both businesses and law firms -- are heading in terms of marketing and research. But, while social media is a great resource to connect with your clients and prospects, it should be only part of your marketing mix -- not your only means of marketing.

This leads me to the next point – HAVE A PLAN! While the tools are free, and you can easily jump on the Internet today and register on the various websites, it is best to play around and get a feel for them before you "go live" with your firm name on the material. If you are forming a plan for your direct mail campaign, you are going to be meticulous. You should take the same approach with social media.

Now let's discuss some of the social media tools and how they can be used to spread the word about your law firm: YouTube, Blogs, Twitter and Facebook.

Practical Advice. Proven Solutions.
www.PILMMA.org

I'd like to thank Gerry Oginksi for really digging into the importance of online video and also touching on the ins and out of YouTube and how you can use it to market your firm. Since he did such a great job, I'll just focus on the other areas, starting with Blogs.

Blogs

A blog, short for weblog, is a website that has reverse chronological posts. Think of it is an online newspaper in which you are the editor. Everything you post is under your power. That said, there is no exact formula for a successful blog.

Getting a blog is simple. Wordpress.com, blogger.com and typepad.com all provide a free resource for you to build a blog. If you don't have any idea about how to build one that reflects your brand and design, then find a company like Consultwebs.com, which offers these services professionally.

A simple search for "Personal Injury Blog" will result in more than 1.7 million results, so using this tool isn't anything new. But, having a blog that people want to actually log onto and read is where your creativity comes into play. What you post will reflect what you want to do with your blog. Therefore, you need to know your audience.

Do you want to appeal to potential clients where your firm's name and image are in their mind? If this is your game plan, then your material may need to be more relaxed than technical law topics. Potential clients will want some entertainment mixed with their education. Post interesting articles from the web that you think will help them out in everyday life. Keep them interested with amazing pictures or videos. Post something that makes them stay and become enlightened or educated on a subject, whether it's law, life, or something else.

Practical Advice. Proven Solutions.
www.PILMMA.org

Do you want to write on legal topics and position yourself as a leader in opinion on those topics? If so, talk about your life as a lawyer: Things you have seen, what upsets you, and why. Don't hold back on your opinion. If your material and opinion are credible and you ruffle some feathers along the way, someone will notice.

After you have designed your blog, defined your audience, and started writing content, the next step is actually getting people to your blog. The easiest way would be to add a link to your blog on your webpage, assuming you have one. If you e-mail people daily, add the link to the section below your name and contact information. Place it on every piece of direct mail you send. Tell friends that you have started one and ask them to give you feedback. Getting people to your blog is like any other type of marketing. The first thing you need to do is let people know you have one.

Here's one main rule to running a blog. BE CONSISTENT! While your goal should be 1-2 posts a week, you really should be posting daily. Pumping fresh content into your blog will heighten your ranking on Google, show your audience you're committed to expressing your opinion, and show clients that you are committed to providing them with educational information.

To end this section on blogs, I will leave you with this secret: The media (whether television, newspapers, or online) - loves blogs. Nothing builds credibility more than being quoted about a law subject. The higher quality your content is, the better chance you have of being found.

Twitter

If blogs are the father of social media, then Twitter is currently the baby of the family *(when it comes to marketing your law firm, that is. There's also Pinterest, Instagram, and other social media*

Practical Advice. Proven Solutions.
www.PILMMA.org

sites that are gaining popularity every day but when it comes to legal marketing, blogs, Twitter, Facebook and YouTube are a tight family.) Twitter is basically a toned down version of a blog, or a microblog, if you will, that asks the user one question upon logging on, "What are you doing?" Twitter is defined as:

A free social networking and micro-blogging service that allows its users to send and read other users' updates (otherwise known as tweets), which are text-based posts of up to 140 characters in length.

To sculpt a mental image of exactly what Twitter is, think of it as sending a text message and the people who receive it have decided to follow what you say. At the core, that is all it is, one big chat room of people telling other people what they are doing and people responding back to what they "tweet" (the official term for sending a twitter message), favoriting the tweet, retweeting the post or mentioning the post and in turn mentioning the person who posted it. So, how does this help you as a lawyer? It gets your name out there and gives you a channel to display your chops as a law firm.

You can tweet anything your heart desires. Did you publish a new blog post? Then tweet about it and see how many people read it and respond. Did you just go to a baseball game? Tweet about it and see how many others may be fans of the same team. Do a Twitter search and see what's trending – use hashtags (#) and post relevant content on a topic that people seem to want to talk about at a given time and it will get picked up when others do searches.

While you want to stay in the professional realm at all times, social media allows you to loosen your tie and show people that you are a person or law firm with interests. People like interesting people. People want to do business with interesting and passionate people. There is no rule that says you can't be passionate about something other than being a lawyer.

Facebook

Since being founded in 2004, Facebook has grown incredibly. By the end of its first year, Facebook had one million active monthly users. In its early days, Facebook was skewed towards a younger crowd due to members needing a college e-mail address to sign up for their services. From a business standpoint they were leaving all kinds of people out of the mix, so they opened the doors to everyone. So if you thought Facebook was just for teens and college kids, think again. Since January 2011, users between the ages of 25-55+ grew a whopping 155%!

As of May 2014, there were 1.28 billion Facebook users. According to data from comScore, time spent on Facebook in the US grew by 500 basis points to 15.8% since 2012. Facebook is ranked the number 1 web property in the US where users spend their time and stands at 1.28 billion users strong as of May 2014.

How can you use Facebook for your firm?

Facebook is best used like a newsletter to your marketing list. The main purpose is to 1) Keep top of mind awareness of who you are and what you do. 2) Build relationships by sharing parts of your life that show that you are a real likeable person and not some stuffed shirt lawyer.

Remember, people refer cases to lawyers they know, like and trust! Use your Facebook posts to accomplish this along with a written newsletter.

When creating a Facebook page you want to stay as professional as possible, while showing that you actually have a life. Fill in your interests and seek out friends from past and present. Be as interesting a person online as you are offline. If you are not interesting, well, there are other books that can help you with that.

Practical Advice. Proven Solutions.
www.PILMMA.org

When you log on, you can announce what you are doing, highlight and link to recent blog posts, tell a story of a case, and so on. If you announce that you have a new blog post, send the link, and if 5 out of your 250 friends/contacts read it, then it's successful.

And last, having a Facebook page allows you to be in the mix and builds your SEO. It allows for one more website that has your image, contact information, and a summary of what you and/or your law firm are all about. One word of advice, do not allow friends to tag pictures of you to be seen by any of your other friends or visitors to your page. All it takes is one picture of you doing something a little risqué to ruin the whole Facebook party.

Sum of All Parts:

In case the advantages of these tools haven't sunk in yet, let me take you through a scenario.

Dale Jones, 27, gets in a car accident and needs representation. He doesn't know where to go so he asks around for referrals to a lawyer. He gets two suggestions from friends at work, your law firm and your competitor's law firm. Mr. Jones is familiar with both names because he received direct mail from both law firms. He goes home and throws everything else away except the direct mail pieces from you and your competitor.

Mr. Jones looks at the direct mail and neither "wows" him more than the other. So he decides to research more. He jumps online to check out each law firm's website. This is where the separation begins. Mr. Jones knows exactly what a blog is, therefore, upon logging onto your website he sees that you have one and he checks it out. In the blog all you're doing is providing helpful information. You're not trying to drag people in with cookie-cutter posts about car wrecks in the town that your law firm is near. Hell, you might even have something funny on there.

Practical Advice. Proven Solutions.
www.PILMMA.org

The blog portrays the firm as a person and Mr. Jones feels like he knows you.

He notices on your blog that you have a Twitter page. He checks out what you have been talking about. He sees only things of educational and entertainment value, pounding in his head that you want to help and you are there to help. He keeps seeing that logo, keeps seeing your face -- the firm is in his mind.

So, Mr. Jones hops onto Google and does a quick search for your name and name only. He's tired of seeing propaganda; he wants to see what you're all about. What comes up? Your Facebook page, which leads him to a page that shows you actually have interests. It shows that you want to be part of the conversation. He sees you like Chinese food. He likes Chinese food. This is getting better and better.

After he clicks out of Facebook, he goes back to Google to see what else came up. He sees that you have a lot of YouTube videos. His attention is drawn to one specifically about car accidents. He also checks the 20 videos of your clients who believed so much in your service that they agreed to appear on camera and talk about how you helped them.

This guy is literally excited to call you. So he checks your competitor just like he checked you. Nothing -- no blog, no Facebook, no YouTube, no Twitter.

Who do you think will get the first call?

Practical Advice. Proven Solutions.
www.PILMMA.org

CHAPTER 11:

Mobile Phones
As Marketing Tools

It was estimated in 2009 that 2.5 billion text messages were sent every day in the US. In 2011, more than 2 trillion SMS messages were sent!

The love affair with text messaging shows no signs of cooling off.

With that said, if you're thinking that mobile phones are still just for making calls on the move or shooting a text here and there, and have no place in marketing your firm – if what I mentioned above hasn't caused you to think differently, the next statistics I share with you will. Honestly, these statistics are truly amazing:

1) It takes 26 hours for the average person to report a lost wallet. It takes 68 minutes for them to report a lost phone. (Source: Unisys)

2) There are 6.8 billion people on the planet. 5.1 billion of them own a cell phone, but only 4.2 billion own a toothbrush. (Source: Mobile Marketing Association Asia)

3) It takes 90 minutes for the average person to respond to an email. It takes 90 seconds for the average person to respond to a text message. (Source: CTIA.org)

4) 70% of all mobile searches result in action within 1 hour. (Source: Mobile Marketer)

5) There are more mobile phones on the planet than there are TVs. (Source: Jupiter)

6) 91% of all U.S. citizens have their mobile device within reach 24/7. (Source: Morgan Stanley)

Demographically speaking, teenagers text more than any other group. Nielsen company research shows that the 18-24 year old is the next biggest texting demographic followed by 25-34 year olds.

The opportunity for mobile marketing is exploding. Portio Research predicts mobile subscribers worldwide will reach 7.5 billion by the end of 2014 and 8.5 billion by the end of 2016.

Practical Advice. Proven Solutions.
www.PILMMA.org

According to data shared by Forbes editor Lewis Dvorkin, of 49 million Forbes.com visitors in July, 40% of views of the most popular post came from smartphones. Mobile is increasingly becoming the primary point of engagement between consumers and brands.

Not sure what to do or how to get started with mobile marketing? There are five priorities to focus on when it comes to mobile marketing. However, for legal mobile marketing, two out of the five are your heavy hitters.

The five priorities are:

1) A unique, branded mobile app

2) Redeemable Deals

3) Event Notification

4) Loyalty

5) Customer Referrals

Of the above, a unique, branded mobile app and client referrals are where it's at for marketing your law firm.

A law firm mobile app should give the consumer a reason to download it. Just making it all about you and your law firm is a waste of your time and dollars.

At Hardison & Cochran we developed an app to help consumers who might have the misfortune of being involved in an automobile crash. We included the following features:

• Click to call

• Highway Patrol telephone numbers

• Get a tow truck

• Cabs

• Accident Hotline – *Click to Call Our Office!*

Practical Advice. Proven Solutions.
www.PILMMA.org

- We also included a Law Cam to take photos at the accident scene as well as a Witness Recorder to get the contact information and statements of those who witnessed the accident if possible.

- We included a Quick Tips section detailing what to do and what not to do at the scene of the accident.

- Another feature focuses on information about what to do days after the accident, including calling your insurance company.

- To get teens involved, we included a Teen Drivers section, giving information on distracted driving. This in addition to a section for parents called "The 6 Steps to Help Your Teenagers Become Safer, More Attentive Drivers".

So you get the idea? The app is 80% about giving consumers a reason to download the app because of useful tools and information and 20% is self-promotion. People are going to expect a little self-promotion but the key to it is to keep it minimal.

The second key to using a mobile phone for marketing is getting referrals. Get referrals by having a "Share" button on your app and educate your app users to share this information and app with all their friends and family. This will help build your mobile app referral network!

Geo-targeting

Geo-targeting in geomarketing and Internet marketing is the method of determining the geolocation of a website visitor and delivering different content to that visitor based on his or her location, such as country, region/state, city, metro code/zip code, organization, IP address, ISP, or other criteria. Using this added technique along with your PPC campaign can improve your ROI if you're willing to be creative and put some thought into it.

Practical Advice. Proven Solutions.
www.PILMMA.org

There are several ways to geo-target, which can be mixed and matched to some extent.

- City, state, county, region
- DMA (Designated Market Area)
- ZIP code
- Radius around a point (ERs for accidents, SSA Office for Disability for claims)
- Location extension targeting

Basically Google will determine what content and which ad to show to the users based on location cues, such as search terms, the physical location of the user and the domain they are viewing. The advanced setting of "People in, searching for, or viewing pages about my targeted location" allows ads to be shown to people who have used the name of the location in their searches or viewed content about your location or selected your location in their search settings.

Geo-targeting with a mobile focus is especially useful for your mobile audience. Using click to call is critical to this since you can geo-target users if they are in your surrounding area and need an attorney. If they search for help, there you will be and all they have to do is click to call and you're on the line.

With geo-targeting, you can even use the weather to help you target your prospective clients. For instance, you'd want to be sure you were focusing on rainy areas for accidents, slip and falls, etc. You can even go as far as increasing your bid on rainy days when the accidents are even more likely to happen!

Practical Advice. Proven Solutions.
www.PILMMA.org

CHAPTER 12:

Television

Television has always been the top medium for lawyer advertising. This remains true today for several reasons. Television casts the "widest net". Television is one of the few mediums that touches everyone. All of our law firms' potential clients own, have access to, and watch television. No other medium can boast the same effect.

I predicted that TV would lose its effectiveness in my first edition of this book back in 2009.

I was right.

Why is T.V. steadily losing its effectiveness for a great majority of law firms? There are 5 main reasons for this, or better yet, 5 dangerous trends facing lawyers who advertise on TV.

Dangerous Trend #1

Traditional TV viewership is declining. The top 20 shows in the 1979-1980 TV seasons had a household rating of 21.7. The top 20 shows in 2009-2010 only had a household rating of 13. Total viewership of the 4 top broadcast networks is down 42% since 1994 according to Brad Agate, Sr. Vice-President of Research at Horizon Media.

Dangerous Trend #2

Since the Bates decision in 1977, TV advertising by PI lawyers has dramatically increased. In the 15 years that followed Bates, expenditures on attorney TV advertising increased from $100 thousand to $114 million in 1992. (Cutler p.1)

By the start of the 21st century, TV advertising outlays totaled over $236 million (Kanter- TNS). This number increased to approximately $493 million in 2009.

There are 2 things to gather from this: 1) Viewership is down overall on the major broadcast stations. Cable TV has changed viewership and fragmented it to such a degree that the effectiveness of TV advertising is decreasing. 2) More and more lawyers are investing in TV advertising which is saturating the market, while at the same time the numbers of personal injury claims are decreasing as cars become safer.

Dangerous Trend #3

I am an avid fan of keeping statistics on what my return on investment is on every expenditure I make for each marketing tactic used to market our law firm. This is why we completely cut the Yellow Pages four years ago – due to the Internet, the cost per case had gone from $400 per case in 1996 to over $2000 per case in 2006.

What our statistics have steadily shown is that there is a trend that the cost per case is increasing each year as more and more lawyers enter the market and viewership becomes more and more fragmented.

I have always been convinced that TV advertising makes lawyers lazy when it comes to marketing. It was always so easy to just put any kind of ad on TV and watch the phones ring off the hook immediately.

That is not the case in today's market. There are numerous firms that have solidly branded themselves over the past 10-20 years and have the lion's share of the market. The fact that there are less cases and more advertising dollars being spent shrinks the market share for each new lawyer who enters the TV advertising market and also decreases the share of the leader of the pack in that TV market. Reaction so far has been for many of the leaders to increase their spending budgets which only tends to increase the cost per case. Based on my own experience, you hit a point

Practical Advice. Proven Solutions.
www.PILMMA.org

in spending on TV advertising that creates a diminishing return. You get more cases but at a much greater cost!

Dangerous Trend #4

What is also interesting is the significant decline in the value of a soft tissue case over the last 10-15 years with the introduction of Colossus by Allstate, which is now being used by the majority of major insurance liability auto carriers.

Insurance carriers are making trial lawyers try the soft tissue cases more and more as time passes. Over the last 7 years, our firm has seen the percentage of cases we file suit on increase from 23% to 42%. The alternative is to take lower settlements and get lower fees, going to suit on soft tissue cases is almost always a losing proposition. Then there is also the cost of loss of time. A wise lawyer once told me *"You don't make money in the courtroom."* Based on my 32 years of experience, this is generally a true statement.

This trend is growing and I see no signs of it going away.

Dangerous Trend #5

With the advent of TIVO and DVRs, many viewers are taping their favorite shows and bypassing commercials entirely. This once could only be afforded by the upper income demographics. As it is always with technology, the longer it is on the market, the cheaper it becomes. Now our target market of middle and lower income families can afford the same TIVO and DVR capabilities as everyone else. You need to start worrying if you haven't already, because it is only going to get worse, not better.

In the near future, the game will change. The TV screen will convert into one that can deliver both TV and Internet content. Many consumers will be able to access their online life with a TV remote and the big screen will behave like a touchscreen. It will know which shows we like and which ones we don't, similar to the technology we have today only much more personalized and evolved.

The TV screen will in essence just become another monitor. Forester Research forecasts that viewers will be able to watch a show on TV for a while, then pick it up on their PC or mobile phone when they leave the house.

What does this mean for you?

Market share is shrinking for the 80-90% of lawyers who advertise on TV. The cost per case is increasing even though the average fee is declining for most law firms. I challenge you to review what your average fee is and what the average cost per case is. To not do so is fiscal suicide on your part. If you look back over the last 5 years, you will see that your average cost per case has increased, while your return on investment has decreased. Client acquisition cost is going to continue to increase each and every year from here on out.

Smart lawyers are the ones who don't ignore this phenomenon. You must make your investment count! You, as a business person, must rigidly control everything, big or small, that happens once consumers raise their hands and follow the calls to action on your TV ads.

What percentage of your annual marketing budget is allocated to TV? I guarantee the answer is more than 50% of your budget. Let's face it, as stated earlier, TV has made you lazy! As the cost per case goes up, you try to grab the next shiny object. If it doesn't work within 90 days, you stop and go to the next shiny object. As mentioned before, continually doing this and being unaware of your ROI is economic suicide.

What can you do to increase the effectiveness of your TV advertising campaign?

TV advertising is not dead and it's not gone. To be more cost effective, you must do certain things in the future or you will fall by the wayside. The following are a few things you can do to increase the effectiveness of your TV ads.

1) Demand Posting from your TV Advertising Agency

Posting is making sure that you get what you bargained for. When TV stations sell you or your agency ad space for your TV commercials, they base the price on the ratings and the number of eyes that are watching your commercial during the time slot you bought. The fact that you might pay $400 for one commercial and $20 for another commercial does not mean that the $20 commercial is cheaper. If you only have 500 sets of eyes watching the $20 commercials and 20,000 sets of eyes watching the $400 commercial, then you can clearly see that the cost per thousand eyes is much, much less with the $400 buy even though it costs you more money.

The TV stations use Nielson ratings and historical data to project how many eyes and what kind of ratings you are going to get from airing your TV commercial during a particular time slot. They charge you based on these assumptions. But that's the problem, these are just assumptions.

To ensure that you are getting what you pay for, your agency should be posting your TV buy.

Posting entails them getting the actual Nielson ratings of the show after it actually airs and comparing the number of eyes and the ratings points it actually earned compared to what you paid for.

You want to negotiate 100% delivery but at no time do you want to accept less than 90%. By doing this the TV stations are held accountable and if they do not meet this criteria then they have to give you your money back or most commonly they will do "make goods" and supplement with extra commercial spots to make-up for the viewership that you were promised but didn't receive.

This can be easily done by your ad agency. If you do not have an ad agency there are companies out there, and even software you can buy, that will do it for you. Last year, our law firm got an extra 700 commercials run because some of the stations under delivered. In one instance we had one TV station that had over 400 TV commercials just to "make good" for their under delivery weight.

2) Create a USP

As I've mentioned various times, with all the proliferation of TV advertising by lawyers on the airways, you must stand out from your competition. The viewer needs to know why they should hire you over all the other lawyers that are on TV or why they need a lawyer at all.

You must remember that potential clients don't care about you! They want to know *"What's in it for me?"* Subconsciously, when people are exposed to advertising materials, they ask themselves a series of questions, *"Why should I do business with that law firm?"*; *"Why shouldn't I call the last lawyer I saw instead?"*; *"Do I even need a lawyer?"*

The purpose of your USP is to answer that question with a response that steers them toward your firm. Refer back to the chapter on USPs if you feel like you need more information on how to create a USP for your firm or simply visit www.CreateAUSP.com

Practical Advice. Proven Solutions.
www.PILMMA.org

3) Create Better Ads

The best TV ads are the ones that catch your eye and hold it. There must be something in the ad that really stands out. You need an ad that is so intriguing that the listeners will unmute their TVs to hear what is going along with the bizarre images on the screen. Better yet, as they are fast forwarding, you want your ad to make them stop and rewind to see what the ads are saying.

Another very important part of a great ad is having an effective headline. You must be able to tell people what you want them to know in 3.2 seconds. The headline should give a benefit and focus on the prospect by using "you" and "your" instead of focusing on yourself by using the word "we". It should communicate the message clearly and want you to stay and listen to find out more. It is important to use your USP in your TV ad. After your headline hooks the viewers, the rest of your copy and graphics will keep them watching.

4) Include a Call to Action

People love to be told what to do. Any commercial that does not have a call to action telling them exactly what to do when they get through watching the TV ad is wasted money. Certain types of calls to action are as follows: "Go to our website," "Download our free report," "Call us now for a free audit of your case," "Pick up the phone and call us 24/7". The key is to tell them what to do and how to do it.

5) Test, Test, Test

To ensure that you are getting the best return on investment with your TV ads and TV buy, you must test your buy and your ads. There is an old famous saying that says, "I know 50% of my marketing is working, I just don't know which 50%." In today's day and age, this does not have to be the rule of thumb.

When you are cutting your TV commercials, it is very easy to rent or buy different 800 numbers and tag each different commercial for each different show or at least each different TV station for tracking purposes. There are even companies out there that will do it for you. The simple truth is that it can still be done, just on a limited basis. You can rent these numbers for 30-60 days and test them in each commercial and on each TV station and then go back to using your vanity numbers.

I know some of you are thinking it will hurt your brand. I know for a fact one lawyer does this every year and spends millions of dollars on his TV ad campaign but tests it for at least 30-60 days using different 800 tracking numbers to evaluate the effectiveness of his ads and TV buys.

Does it cost more? Yes, it does. But in the long run it is a lot cheaper than running an ineffective ad or making an ineffective TV buy.

6) Create Systems and Scripts for Intake Personnel

At PILMMA, we have instituted a service for our upper echelon members. This is a ghost calling service where we mystery shop our members' law firms with a fake call, record it, and then use it as training for their staff. What amazes me is that some of the largest firms in our group that have the largest marketing budgets do so poorly when it comes to converting new leads from TV advertising into new cases. By scripting and using these mystery phone calls as training tapes for their staff and lawyers, our members have increased their conversion rates by significant numbers.

7) Create Systems for Following-up on Leads

Another thing I constantly see in touring the country and talking to lawyers, especially in my consulting business, is that lawyers have no follow-up procedures or systems in place for new callers

Practical Advice. Proven Solutions.
www.PILMMA.org

that may not convert on the first call. To give up this easily and not pursue the potential new clients any further is a big waste of your advertising dollars. The key to it is that you must have a system in place and benchmarks to ensure that the procedures or systems are being implemented by your staff.

One way is to create a series of e-mail auto-responders or follow-up mailings giving the potential new clients more information, such as helpful consumer guides and reports that will position you as the *"Go-To Attorney – The Expert!"*

Basically, you are using Educational Based Marketing to convert those leads without trying to look desperate and sell yourself. You can do this by offering free reports on things like how to handle property damage. One that we have had very good success with is "7 Fatal Mistakes Accident Victims of NC Make and How to Avoid Making Them". This book has converted many new callers into new cases. Many of the members of PILMMA have created their own consumer books as well on disability, workers comp; auto accidents, slip and falls, and product liability cases and they have all been very successful in converting leads without selling.

While TV is still presently an important role in advertising for large personal injury firms, the Internet and cell phone technology will become King and TV will be Queen within the next 5-10 years. So my advice to you is to follow the tips above and diversify your marketing tactics to create a truly effective marketing strategy for your firm.

Practical Advice. Proven Solutions.
www.PILMMA.org

CHAPTER 13:

Yellow Pages – Why They Don't Work Anymore

Within the next 5 years, Yellow Pages will be completely obsolete. It is arguable that this hasn't happened already. Yellow Page response rates are steadily declining. Fewer people are using them every year. At the same time, the monthly cost to maintain your same size ad continues to rise.

During the 80's and early 90's, Yellow Page advertising was a very effective form of marketing your law firm. Very few lawyers advertised on TV. The Internet was not available to the general public and, until the break-up of "Ma Bell" in 1994, there was only one phone directory. All of these factors made advertising in the Yellow Pages very cost effective.

Since 1994, there has been a steady decline in the effectiveness of Yellow Page advertising. This ineffectiveness has been more widespread in certain geographic areas and has rapidly increased in the past 4-5 years. There are several reasons for this. Today, more and more lawyers are spending more on TV advertising. The increasing use of vanity numbers such as 1-800-Lawyers, 1-800-HURT911, and 1-800-HURTNOW means fewer people need to look up phone numbers. There has also been an influx of Yellow Page directories. Some markets have anywhere from 2-5 directories. All of these factors have substantially reduced the return on investment for Yellow Page advertising.

The Internet has had the biggest impact by far on Yellow Page return. First, most people searching for any type of business will search online for contact information and to perform research. A growing percentage of people can even search for phone numbers on their cell phones. Also, the Yellow Page directory companies know that their large books are becoming a thing of the past! Many directories such as "The Yellow Book", "AT&T – The Real Yellow Pages", and "Verizon – Superpages" have invested millions of dollars on the Internet and are now pushing pay per clicks and banner ads on their online sites to supplement their declining Yellow Page print revenues.

According to Verizon's own internal marketing division, if a person already knows who they want to call, 80% go to the white pages to find the number. Based on my experience and research, a majority of Yellow Page "callers" are either price shoppers – or, as I like to call them, "tire kickers". This is someone who has already been turned down by 4-5 previous attorneys because they don't have a case.

Today, for consumers to use the Yellow Pages they must:

1) Not have a name in mind

2) Not have been recommended to a firm by a friend or neighbor

3) Not have Internet access (75% of Americans do have access)

All of these things must happen simultaneously in order for someone to utilize the Yellow Pages to "search" for an attorney. So, as you can clearly see, Yellow Pages are slowly but surely becoming a dying medium for lawyer advertising.

However, Yellow Page ads do work in some markets. The more rural the market, the better chance you have of actually getting a reasonable return on your Yellow Page investment.

Practical Advice. Proven Solutions.
www.PILMMA.org

CHAPTER 14:

The Future of Print

Direct Mail

Although some state bars have limited or completely eliminated direct mail, it remains one of the most cost effective means of acquiring new clients. Direct mail, unlike Yellow Pages, will still be around well into the 21st century. As long as post offices, stamps, and the desire to send and receive mail as a means of communication continue to exist, direct mail will be here. There are some rumblings of establishing "DO NOT MAIL" lists as was done for the telemarketers in the establishment of "DO NOT CALL" lists. I believe this law will not pass because the lobby for direct mail is too strong.

Today, the technology exists where you can use direct mail in conjunction with the Internet. This technology is called PURL (Personalized URL). Personalized URLs are a way to personalize web pages to specific prospects. The name of the prospect is inserted into the front of the URL. When the person enters their personalized URL into their web browser, the page they see is customized to them. This technology used to be somewhat cost prohibitive, but now it is completely affordable and cost effective.

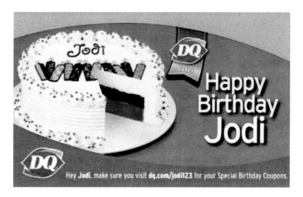

PURLs have the unique ability to take an inexpensive direct mail media like post cards (where the space is limited) and drive potential clients to the web, where the space is unlimited and virtually free.

Practical Advice. Proven Solutions.
www.PILMMA.org

Here is how it works:

You send direct mail postcards to a targeted list of prospects. You ask them to go to a specific website (one you have created specifically for them, such as www.JohnDoe.29Tactics.com) that upon visiting will greet them with their name. You then ask them to answer a few questions and give their email address for a free report, which prequalifies them. You can run all sorts of reports on this information and track who visited your website and how they answered the questions.

Think of the possibilities. You could follow-up with an auto-responder and about 4-10 e-blasts to these prospects. Auto-responders are pre-scripted emails that automatically blast out through the use of CRM software (Client Relationship Marketing). It is only a matter of time before the lawyers who already use direct mail will latch onto it. Then it will really take off.

Newsletters

Newsletters are often overlooked as an effective marketing tool for lawyers. Referrals from former clients and callers are the very best source for new cases. Newsletters build a fence around your past clients. A newsletter that is sent out on a monthly basis keeps your law firm at the top of their minds. When someone they know needs a lawyer – your firm is the first one out of their mouths!

Top of mind awareness is so important. I tell lawyers who don't have a large budget to do a newsletter even if you don't or can't do anything else. A newsletter is the way to go.

Newsletters also help with branding. You want people to remember who you are and what you do. They help build a continued relationship with past clients. These clients get to know you and "keep in touch" with you and your firm on a more personal level – as long as it's an effective newsletter!

Practical Advice. Proven Solutions.
www.PILMMA.org

An effective newsletter's content should be less than one-third about law. It should also:

1) Be client focused

2) Give great value

3) Be informative, fun, and easy to read

4) Be readable in 10 minutes and written on a 5th-6th grade reading level.

5) Be frequent and dependable

People love humor. Use this to keep them interested in your newsletter. You can even include a monthly joke about lawyers to keep it lighthearted and friendly. Stay away from the legal mumbo jumbo and make it consumer-based by including tips and relevant information.

Clients and former clients want to know more about you and others in your law firm. They want to make a connection.

Your list of clients is vital to your firm. If you don't stay in touch with them and make that connection, you risk losing them to your competition. Look, your list is so important, that Ben Glass once said if you took all of his marketing and only left him with one thing, he hoped that it would be his newsletter and e-zine list.

And I agree.

You can do them yourself or have a vendor do them for you. There are several vendors who do newsletters such as Premier Print Marketing, www.premierprintmarketing.com.

I am often asked where to find content if you do your newsletter in-house. We use www.FirstDraft.biz. They send you monthly articles on an array of subjects, along with puzzles, humorous anecdotes, and jokes. You can choose to use them as is, or add

Practical Advice. Proven Solutions.
www.PILMMA.org

copy to them and make them your own. Either way, it's a great resource for copy and a heck of a time saver.

But whatever you do, don't start a newsletter that is sporadic in its publication. People really get used to them and look forward to reading about your firm! Like everything in marketing, BE CONSISTENT!

CHAPTER 15:

Radio

Radio is the second most powerful medium in the US, reaching 59% of the population daily. In comparison, Internet reaches 49% while print media accounts for only 13%. While radio was one of the earliest forms of mass media and still remains a popular medium, its audience has slowly been eroding due to the Internet, TV, iPods, and recently, subscription-based satellite radio like SiriusXM.

Online radio is used by more than 15% of American radio listeners but is expected to continue to increase its reach with the extensive growth of and reliance on the Internet and mobile devices in the US.

Altogether, American radio stations brought in $15.1 billion in revenue in 2012. Of this, $510 million was generated online. With that being said, it's not a surprise to learn that 45% of Americans trust radio advertising according to Nielsen.

According to eMarketer, Internet radio ad spending in the US was projected to reach $970 million in 2013 and grow to $1.31 billion by 2016.

Radio is good if you are trying to reach a narrow demographic. Also, radio is super easy to track with repeater numbers such as 800-600-7535.

Most lawyers love vanity numbers like "1-800- CALL KEN". I personally think they are overrated for several reasons.

First, it limits your ability to use different numbers to track your marketing effectiveness. Secondly, nearly all the good vanity numbers are taken and the only way you can get them is to lease them. On the other hand, repeater numbers can be purchased relatively cheaply compared to the price you'd have to pay to obtain a vanity number.

Based on the above, I am a large proponent of buying repeater numbers and using a different one for each different ad used on radio and TV to track the effectiveness of each ad.

CHAPTER 16:

Client Relationship Marketing and Referral Marketing

What exactly is Client Relationship Marketing as it relates to your law firm? Client Relationship Marketing (CRM) is the process of marketing your law firm by nurturing your relationship with your existing clients while providing an exceptional client experience. These clients then become your cheerleaders and will refer your firm to countless future clients.

Who is responsible for CRM in your firm? EVERYONE, from the mail clerk to the managing partner. You must create an environment within your firm that promotes the fact that everyone is responsible for marketing the firm. They are all in this together and must take responsibility for the firm's success.

Here's the key: you don't just want satisfied clients -- you want loyal clients. You want clients who will always refer your firm to their family and friends. You want clients who will sing your praises and give you written and verbal testimonials.

You should couple a client loyalty program with some quality assurance standards and hold people accountable. In my firm, for example, we talk to every client once every sixty days -- and every client receives an update letter every thirty days. Sound impossible? Absolutely not. I had a program designed that shows me the case name, status of the case, the last time an attorney talked to the client, and the last time the case manager talked to the client. They are required to have a 90% or better success rate. If they don't, they are given thirty days to pull it into line -- and if they don't, they receive a written warning with the consequences spelled out. To emphasize the importance of client loyalty even more, I tie bonuses in my firm directly to client service.
Only you can decide where to spend your marketing dollars. And, only you can decide the return on your investment. I have often said that my name is my most valuable asset, and my marketing program keeps my name out in front as one who puts his clients first. The return on this investment is immeasurable!

Practical Advice. Proven Solutions.
www.PILMMA.org

The Importance of Client Loyalty

Today's lawyer is so focused on getting the message out that will persuade the potential client to call the firm, that the lawyer fails to look within to see if a change in the thought process, management, or delivery of the product can create new clients. As someone who spends a great deal of money on marketing, I have become quite savvy on how to generate free clients.

Traditionally, the client used to have one lawyer who handled everything. Then, due to fast-paced technology, coupled with a much smarter client, lawyers could not depend on repeat business. The advent of lawyers doing marketing by touting cheaper rates or other hooks knocked the old-time family lawyer right off the top rung. Those lawyers today are still trying to figure out what went wrong and how to change their practices to meet the 21st Century's client consumer.

Today's firm marketing has to be more than Yellow Pages, television, or other media markets. Firms must figure out what the client wants and deliver it in such a fashion that they become *mini-marketers* for your law firm.

Today's client wants more than just a lawyer. I don't recall one client who has asked me where I went to law school, what my class ranking was, or even if they could see my law license. Clients were looking for me to get on their level, talk to them, and be available to them.

I'm a keeper of statistics, and it became apparent when we implemented our strategic plan back in 1997 that my most valuable commodity was my high rate of client rapport. A good portion of my business came from clients who genuinely liked me, and told everyone about me long after their case was settled.

Over the years, I started noticing that there was a big difference between 'just satisfying' the client with the right results, and

Practical Advice. Proven Solutions.
www.PILMMA.org

developing a relationship with the client that lasted far beyond the settlement of the case. Thus, I created and designed a client loyalty program within my firm that accounts for approximately 44% of my new clients, many of which were referred by clients I represented over 15 years ago. Ask anyone at my firm and they will agree that my development of client loyalty versus client satisfaction is non-negotiable. I don't care how much money you generate, you must create client loyalty.

CLIENT LOYALTY IS NOT THE SAME THING AS CLIENT SATISFACTION!!!

Excellent service leads to client satisfaction, which is an essential element in creating client loyalty. But a client can be satisfied with the results and still feel no personal tie to you or your firm.

The concept of client loyalty includes five things:

1. The client's overall satisfaction when doing business with a law firm.
2. The client's willingness to build a relationship with you and your company.
3. The client's willingness to be a repeat client.
4. The client's willingness to recommend you to others.
5. The client's reluctance to switch to another law firm.

CLIENT TURNOFFS:

Client turnoffs arise when employees (and I mean both lawyers and non-lawyers) fail to communicate well, both verbally and non-verbally. Some examples of client turnoffs are:

1. Failure to greet or even smile at a client.
2. Failure to see the client on time.
3. Inaccurate information given or lack of knowledge conveyed.
4. Failure to give full attention to the client either while on the phone or when meeting them in person.
5. Rude or uncaring attitude.

6. Inappropriate, dirty, or sloppy appearance at the workplace.
7. Any communicative message that causes the client to feel uncomfortable.

Surveys completed by the U.S. Office of Consumer Affairs revealed these interesting facts (within this book, client and customer are interchangeable):

1. One client in four is dissatisfied with some aspect of a typical transaction.
2. Only 5% of dissatisfied clients complain to the company. The vast silent majority would rather switch than fight. They simply take their business elsewhere.
3. A dissatisfied client will tell 10 to 20 people (12 is the average) about a company that provided poor service. Some people will tell hundreds or even thousands.

How does this affect our business? If 25% of our clients are unhappy or unhappy with our service, but only 5% of that 25% bother to complain, the impact can be devastating.

Let's take a typical injury law firm that signs up 1000 clients per year. If 250 clients are unhappy but we hear from only 5% of that 250, which is approximately 13, that may sound good to everyone until they realize that the 237 quiet ones are likely to tell 2,844 people (237 x 12 = 2,844). Adversely, if a client is completely satisfied, he might tell 1 to 3 people or an average of 2.

In 2013, our statistics showed us that there were three major sources of clients in our firm, and it broke down as follows:

421 cases or 41% were TV

140 cases or 14% were from our website

340 cases or 33% were from personal referrals

Now let me tell you the cost of getting those referrals. In real dollars, TV cost about $900 per client. The website cost

Practical Advice. Proven Solutions.
www.PILMMA.org

approximately $500 per case to get them in the front door. And last but not least, personal referrals cost absolutely nothing. Which type of referral do you think I want?

What is also important to note is that of the 340 personal referrals that we signed up, we received 823 referrals, which means that we had a 41% success rate in signing up personal referrals. In TV advertising, we had 2,333 calls and signed up 421 new cases. This was a conversion rate of 18%. Our website yielded 1,268 inquiries and only 140 sign-ups, which is only an 11% conversion rate. You can clearly see that the personal referrals are already sold on our services when they seek us out. They're not just shopping around for attorneys or trying to find out information. They come to us wanting our services. This also costs the firm less time and money in converting these calls to actual cases. Now I ask you, which do you think is the most cost effective form of marketing we do in the firm and also yields us the greatest conversion rate? It is clear…the personal referrals from our past clients and people we do business with.

Now let's go to the actual dollar cost of an unhappy client. As I stated earlier, out of 1000 clients, if we go by the national average, we have about 250 unhappy clients. Of those 250 clients, 95% never express discontent, but also never come back or refer any clients either. Thus, we have 237 people who could have spoken to at least 474 people and referred us, which on the average would have converted 41% or 196 clients. In actual costs, just look at the following:

If we had to replace these clients with TV advertisements, the cost would be $176,400. But better yet, let's think of the lost income. If we average $4000 a fee and we lose 196 potential clients, then we have lost approximately $800,000 in revenue for the year.

Practical Advice. Proven Solutions.
www.PILMMA.org

BASED ON THE ABOVE, IF WE FOLLOWED THE NATIONAL AVERAGE, LOST REVENUE WOULD BE OVER $1,000,000

Potential clients are bombarded with over 3,000 messages a day meant to influence their spending habits. Whether it's the billboard they pass everyday on the way to work, the label on the bottle of Pepsi they're drinking, or the Cadillac emblem on the car they're stuck behind in traffic, these visual messages are meant to create top of mind awareness and persuade the consumer the next time they're in the market to buy a certain product or service. With the huge number of messages reaching them every day, it's no wonder that consumer buying habits can change at the drop of a hat.

That said, client loyalty is of the utmost importance. Simplistic messages that create top of mind-awareness cannot sway the loyal client. While the competition is spending dollars upon dollars on ways to increase client volume, many of them are forgetting the importance of their existing clients. Forgetting this will almost certainly lead to a number of unsatisfied clients, who will likely never become loyal clients.

In over thirty years of practice, I have learned many things and one of the most important is how to develop client loyalty and keep client loyalty. By following some very common sense rules and setting the stage for all lawyers and employees who work for you, client loyalty is easy to develop. I candidly tell everyone that my practice rises and falls based on client loyalty.

15 SECRETS TO DEVELOPING CLIENT LOYALTY

1. GREET CLIENTS PROMPTLY

A survey clocked the number of seconds people had to wait to be greeted in several businesses. Researchers then asked clients how

Practical Advice. Proven Solutions.
www.PILMMA.org

long they had been waiting. In every case, the client's estimate of the time elapsed was much longer than the actual time. A client waiting 30 or 40 seconds often feels like he or she has been waiting 3 or 4 minutes. Time drags when people are waiting. One of the things we can do to greet clients properly is not to put them on hold and answer the phone on the first ring when you are being paged by the receptionist. The key to greeting clients is simple – *Don't keep them waiting.*

This is a good time to tell you that one of your best investments is a good receptionist or front desk person. This person can make or break your firm simply by not being a people person. Give this person great latitude to get the calls answered and if the rest of the firm doesn't fall in line, afford this person an open door policy with you. I have found time and time again, the person on the front desk knows for a fact whether or not you are meeting client satisfaction goals.

2. APPLY GOOD CONVERSATION SKILLS

A good way to create client rapport is to talk to people like they are in your living room. People in general are intimated by lawyers in law offices. It is your job to make them feel comfortable as they have already been through a traumatic event or they would not be hiring you to start with. Something to use break the ice would be the weather. For example, *"Isn't the sunshine just beautiful?"* or *"Some snowfall, isn't it?"*

Some preferred topics of conversation can be considered *small talk.* Americans prefer to talk about weather, sports, jobs, mutual acquaintance, and past experiences, especially ones they have in common with their conversation partners. Most Americans are taught to avoid discussing politics or religion especially with people they do not know well because these are considered controversial topics.

Practical Advice. Proven Solutions.
www.PILMMA.org

Look for clues to gauge the client's interest. You must understand that interaction means that both parties have an opportunity to participate. If one party monopolizes the conversation, both sides lose.

3. AVOID INAPPROPRIATE CONVERSATION

As a general rule, avoid the following:

1. Criticizing or belittling others
2. Griping about the firm, the department, managers or staff
3. Passing on gossip or hurtful comments about others
4. Using excessive profanity
5. Starting up bad feelings among people
6. Making racial, religious, or gender insults
7. Making comments with sexual undertones and/or overtones

As a general rule, appropriate conversation includes:

1. Making positive and upbeat comments
2. Being supportive of other people
3. Giving others the benefit of the doubt
4. Complimenting freely and often
5. Acknowledgement of people's accomplishments, birthdays, and holidays

4. BUILD RAPPORT WITH THE CLIENT

1. Be a good listener
2. Relate to what they are going through
3. Invite feedback

5. BE SINCERE AND SHOW EMPATHY

We have preached for years that *"But for the grace of God, go I"* and we should understand when working with these people that they are hurting – some are without jobs, without family. That could be us. We need to be sincere in our dealings with our clients and let them know that we do care, we do feel their pain, and we are here to help them.

6. USE GOOD PHONE TECHNIQUES

A key to successful phone use is simply to remember that your client cannot see you. Your challenge is to make up for the lost impact of nonverbal communication by using your voice effectively. The best ways to use the phone effectively are:

1. Give the client your name; let the client know who you are just as you would in a face-to-face situation.

2. Smile into the phone. Believe it or not, people can hear you smile over the phone! Some telephone pros place a mirror in front of them while they are on the phone. Always remember to SMILE.

3. Keep your client informed. If you need to look up information, tell the client what you are doing. Don't leave them holding a dead phone with no clue as to whether you are still with them.

4. Invite the client to get to the point. Use questions such as *"How can I assist you today?"* or *"What can I do for you?"*

5. Commit to the requests of the client. Tell the client specifically what you will do and when you will get back to them.

6. Thank the client. This lets the client know when the conservation is over.

7. Let your voice fluctuate in tone, rate, and loudness. You hold people's attention by putting a little life into your voice. Express honest reactions in expressive ways. Let your voice tone be natural and friendly.

8. Use hold carefully. People hate being put on hold. It is necessary to explain why you are placing them on hold and break in periodically to let them know they haven't been forgotten. If what you are doing will take longer than a few minutes, ask the client if you can call them back. Write down your commitment to call them back and do not forget to do so.

Practical Advice. Proven Solutions.
www.PILMMA.org

9. Use friendly, common, tactful words. Never accuse the client of anything; never convey that their request is an imposition.

7. BE POLITE AT ALL COSTS

Always use the words *please* and *thank you*. I know this isn't brain surgery but it is important. Sometimes the simplest things can make a huge difference in client's perceptions and this is an area where that is the case. Clients want to be appreciated and treating them politely conveys appreciation. Please and Thank You are powerful words for building client rapport and creating client loyalty. They are easy to say and well worth the effort.

8. ENJOY PEOPLE AND THEIR DIVERSITY

Every person is different; each has a unique personality. But the kinds of people who tend to bug us the most are the ones who are not like us. Recognize this, accept diversity and learn to enjoy it. Know that people's needs are basically the same; similarly, when we treat clients like guests, with dignity and courtesy, it creates goodwill.

9. CALL PEOPLE BY THEIR NAMES

People love to hear their names. Think about the times when someone unexpectedly addressed you by your name…didn't it feel good? Didn't you feel less like a number and more like someone who was valued?

People appreciate it when you make the effort to find out and address them by their names. Here are some ways to make the most out of calling clients by their names:

1. When appropriate, introduce yourself to the client and ask his or her name.
2. Avoid being overly familiar too quickly. It's normally safe to call people Mr. Smith or Mrs. Jones, but could be seen as rude if you call them Homer or Marge.

Practical Advice. Proven Solutions.
www.PILMMA.org

3. If you aren't sure how to pronounce the name, ask the client.

4. If a person has an unusual or interesting name, comment on it in a positive way.

5. If a person shares a name with someone in your family or with a friend, comment on that.

People are usually proud of their names and will feel honored when you acknowledge them. Take time to get and use the names of your clients.

10. LISTEN WITH MORE THAN YOUR EARS

Most of us are not good listeners. We listen with 25% of our potential, which means we ignore, forget, distort, or misunderstand 75% of what we hear. Hard to believe, perhaps, but true. Such lazy listening habits can be very costly, both to our businesses and to ourselves. Here are some tips on how to be a better listener:

1. *Resist distractions.* Force yourself to keep your mind on what is being said.

2. *Be an opportunist:* What can I get out of what is being said; how can this information help build a relationship with this client?

3. *Stay Alert:* It is easy to daydream if the speaker is a bit boring or talking very slowly but try to focus. Make the client the center of your attention.

4. *Listen for central themes, relevant and isolated facts:* Too often people get hopelessly lost as listeners because they focus on unimportant facts and details and miss the speaker's main point. Judge the content of what people are saying not the way they are saying it. Clients may not have the right words, but they know what they need better than anyone else.

5. *Listen as though you had to report the content of the message to someone in 8 hours:* This forces you to concentrate and remember. It is a good technique to practice.

6. *Develop note taking skills:* The simple process of typing or writing down key points as you hear them helps you retain what you hear, even if you do not read the notes later.

7. *Hold your fire:* Don't jump to make judgments. Wait until your client has finished talking.

8. *Work on listening:* Tune out those thoughts that get you thinking about something else.

9. *Seek clarification from your client until you fully understand their needs:* One way to do this is to repeat what you think they are trying to say using sincere, open-ended questions.

11. DRESS NEATLY AND APPROPRIATELY

It's true. People do judge you by the way you look. When clients come in our office, we must look professional and our workplace must be clean and neat. People who see sloppy offices think sloppy work. Don't think office image doesn't work. I had a client tell me he hired me because my office looked like I had spent a great deal of money on it and he figured I had to be successful if I could afford to have a nice looking office.

12. WEAR YOUR SMILE WHEN A CLIENT COMES INTO THE OFFICE

Always put on your smile when somebody comes into the office. Be complimentary. Complimenting takes only a second and can add enormous goodwill. If you don't do this very often, get into the habit of saying something complimentary to each of your clients. Safe grounds for sincere compliments are as follows:

1. An article of clothing they are wearing
2. Their children
3. Their behavior
4. Something they own
5. Their helpfulness. For example, *"Thank you for filling out the forms so carefully, that will help."*

Practical Advice. Proven Solutions.
www.PILMMA.org

13. FISH FOR NEGATIVE FEEDBACK

What?! Fish for negative feedback?? Exactly. Negative feedback is the kind that helps us improve. In client service, there is no neutral gear – we either improve or we slip backwards. The best way to get feedback is to let clients know that you really want their honest opinion…good news or bad…and provide ways for them to tell you.

A good way to do this is to use open-ended questions when people express their ideas. An open-ended question cannot be answered with a simple yes or no or one-word response. Below are common questions with one word answers you hear every day in businesses that be easily changed to open-ended questions:

Instead of saying:	Say:
"How was everything?"	"What else can I do for you?"
"Can I get you something else?"	"What else can I get for you?"
"Will that be all?"	"What else can I do for you?"
"Was everything satisfactory?"	"What else could we do better to serve you?"
"Did we meet your needs?"	"How else can we be of service?"

14. THE GRANDMA SELF-TEST

Best-selling author and speaker, Jeffrey Gitomer, passes along this bit of wisdom and I agree with him. This is a sure-fire way to determine how *what you say* will sound to the client. A way to *test your talk* is to put *Grandma* at the end of everything you say. Every time you speak to a client, end it with *Grandma* – if it sounds like something you would say to your grandmother or your grandmother would want to hear, then say it. If not, don't.

For example, how would this sound?
"Sorry, we're closed, Grandma."
"Next! Grandma."
"What is this in reference to Grandma?"
"It's our policy, Grandma."

Practical Advice. Proven Solutions.
www.PILMMA.org

Get it? If you wouldn't say it to your *Grandma*, why would you say it to your client? There are lots of phrases you use every day that irritate clients, and you may have no clue until you insert *Grandma* at the end. Try it and test yourself – take the five phrases you say all the time and add Grandma at the end.

15. LIVE BY THE GOLDEN RULE

I have preached this ever since I started practicing law. Simply put, *Treat people the way you would want to be treated.* Because I believe that these rules are so simple, it constantly amazes me that other law firms do not put them into play. I have come to realize that the leadership of the firm has to set the standards, and these rules as the basis of a client loyalty program have to be non-negotiable. You absolutely 100% must be willing to terminate your highest income producer or your best non-lawyer if they don't believe in client loyalty. I have done it and never regretted it.

THE FINAL CAVEAT

The rules and the thought process sound simple but it truly requires the top leadership to define the program for the rest of the firm. You have to make a client loyalty program non-negotiable with respect to continued employment with your firm. If you allow one person for any reason whatsoever to not be accountable, it simply will not work because your other remaining employees will know you do not truly believe in the program.

I have gone to great lengths to implement my client loyalty philosophy in all aspects of my firm including having a Client Advocate available for dissatisfied or concerned clients, creating and living by a Client Bill of Rights, and utilizing Catalyst's *High Performance Training Classes* for law firms to teach people how to be *people persons*. I no longer hire non-lawyers based on legal experience but rather based on ATTITUDE not aptitude. I will

Practical Advice. Proven Solutions.
www.PILMMA.org

not allow ego driven attorneys in my firm. I do pre-hire testing and I do annual yearly profile testing to see how our people can improve.

The return on the investment – essentially free marketing through client loyalty – is truly priceless.

In closing, I would have to tell you one other side benefit – the unexpected one. Because we are a true client first firm, our work culture has changed. We attract the best of the best and we have a waiting list of people wanting to work with us. It is because we are allowing our people and our clients to establish relationships that give mutual satisfaction to each other.

Client Loyalty has translated into firm loyalty with my employees – work production is high, retention rate is above average, and there is a genuine positive feeling at the office that makes you happy to come to work.

Only you can decide if you or your firm is willing to change – I can only tell you that it works!

The future of your CRM will be influenced by how often you elect to stay in touch with your past clients and prospects. The more touches per year you have -- the more you are kept in front of them for top of mind awareness. How will you do this?

• Postcards
• Print newsletters
• E-zines
• Holiday cards
• Birthday cards
• Voice broadcasting

See website – www.automatedsolutions.com
(Used for sending personal telephone messages from a partner to thousands of past clients in a matter of moments.)

- Handwritten "thank you" cards for referrals.
- Appreciation "events" such as BBQs and concerts.

CRM is not a new concept. It has been around since the beginning of time. Some have called it "customer service". Others have called it public relations. But no matter what you call it, it may be the only way for small firms to survive in the 21st century. With the larger firms spending more and more on marketing and advertising, we should look at how "mom and pop" operations handled the huge conglomerate Wal-Mart coming into their small communities. Look at some of their strategies to see how to compete and thrive -- not merely survive.

PART III:

How to Effectively Market Your Personal Injury Practice in the 21st Century

CHAPTER 17:

Where Do You Start?

Personal Injury firms are usually the victim of salespeople pushing their latest and greatest shiny object. And, most lawyers are so busy practicing law that they don't know whether to try it or not.

What do the successful firms do to know what works without trying it first? They network with other firms and communicate on a regular basis to gain information. How do they do this? Through a process created over seventy years ago by Napoleon Hill. The concept is called a Masterminding.

The successful personal injury law firms have numerous mastermind groups at their disposal, from "Market Masters" and the "M & L Group" to the "CJ Group" and the "Lawyers Marketing Roundtable Group", among numerous others. These groups allow only one law firm/lawyer per TV market, so they can freely share what is and is not working in attracting new clients. For a more detailed explanation of how mastermind groups work, please refer to PILMMA's Mastermind page at www.PILMMA.org/Mastermind.html.

Joining and being part of a mastermind group can help you grow your practice in ways that you can't even imagine. Personally I have been a member of 3 mastermind groups at one time. I attribute much of my wealth and success to being a mastermind. A mastermind group is almost like a fraternity of like-minded lawyers that contribute to each other's success. They openly share new ways to successfully build a law firm without the worry of giving away trade secrets because no member is in the same market as another.

Knowledge is power. Those who can shorten the learning curve by learning from fellow lawyers, who aren't in their market, are lawyers who will rise to the top and be leaders in their markets.

Practical Advice. Proven Solutions.
www.PILMMA.org

CHAPTER 18:

The 6 Marketing Strategies Your Law Firm Must Implement To Compete in the 21st Century

There are many ways smaller personal injury firms can compete and survive the "Wal-Mart Effect" of the mega law firms. We will explore them and I will share what I believe are the six major strategies you will have to implement to compete in the 21st Century.

Strategy #1 – Differentiate Yourself

We discussed the power of setting yourself apart from your competitors by creating a USP. You do this by pushing a unique benefit that no other lawyer in your market has touted. I often hear among lawyers, "We all do the same thing." In many ways that statement is true. But, if you are the first to market a specific benefit, you will stand out above your competition.

This is what is called creating a "Pre-emptive USP" as mentioned back in chapter 2. Back in the 1960's Schlitz Beer touted that their beer bottles were steam cleaned. The fact was that every brewery was steam cleaning their bottles! Schlitz, however, was the first to advertise it as a unique selling proposition. By using it first, they pre-empted their competition from claiming it as their USP. You can do the same thing in your law practice. For example: Helping victims of car accidents get a rental car or handling their property damage claim for free; A social security practice could offer to help complete the initial application for free.

What Wal-Mart survivors have taught us is there are always benefits (not features) that can differentiate your firm from your larger competitors. Finding that unique benefit is easier than you think.

Strategy #2 – Use Education-Based Marketing Methods

Recall from previous chapters, where we discussed the benefits and advantages of Education-Based Marketing. For excellent examples of Education-Based Marketing, please visit www. TreyRyder.com. Trey is the King of helping lawyers implement

Practical Advice. Proven Solutions.
www.PILMMA.org

Education-Based Marketing strategies. He is a genius when it comes to education-based marketing – see Appendix A. "What is Education Based Marketing" – by Trey Ryder.

Here are just a few:

1) Write a consumer book on your practice area – see: www.pilmmapublishing.com.

2) Write free reports and submit them to web article depositories.

    a) Use them in direct mail.

    b) Put them on your website as free downloadable reports.

3) Advertise free copies of your books and reports

    a) On your TV ads

    b) In your radio ads

    c) In your newsletters to other professionals

    d) In your newsletters to past clients

    e) Offer them to prospective clients

4) Offer free seminars on your practice area at local churches, libraries and fairs.

5) Get a booth at local festivals and flea markets and give away your books and free reports.

When you use consumer education-based marketing to attract new clients, you position yourself as the expert and the "Go to Lawyer"!

Strategy #3 – Use the Internet Unmercifully To Attract New Clients

The Internet is the most important marketing weapon a personal injury lawyer has to combat their competitors in the next 20 years! As we discussed, the Internet is the future and the present. The Internet goes hand-in-hand with a consumer education-based marketing plan. Below is a list of specific weapons you need to begin implementing immediately to compete with your competition.

Practical Advice. Proven Solutions.
www.PILMMA.org

1) Create a website chock full of consumer information about your practice areas.

2) Add new informational content monthly if not weekly.

3) Hire an SEO expert to get you on the first page of Google, Yahoo! and Bing.

4) Use pay per click to supplement the SEO of your website.

5) Create a blog and post to it weekly.

6) Use video on your website and also place the video on YouTube.

7) Use Facebook and Twitter to create a following.

8) Collect all the email addresses of your past and current clients as well as all the inquiries of those who didn't hire you so you can send e-blasts and e-zines to stay in the top of their minds and make them your future clients.

9) Create reports and white papers that are free and downloadable to your website visitors.

10) Use Live Chat to instantly engage visitors by answering their questions.

11) Use follow-up sequences on leads you really want to convert into cases. You can implement this with a CRM software system called Infusionsoft. For more information about Infusionsoft, go to https://pilmma.infusionsoft.com/app/page/infusionsoft-special-offer.

Strategy #4 – Implement A Client Relationship Program To Increase Your Client Personal Referrals

The key is to create an exceptional client experience, not just provide good legal and client service. You must create and implement certain quality control systems to ensure that your firm is truly creating an exceptional experience for your clients. Below are some examples of things you should do. The list is not

Practical Advice. Proven Solutions.
www.PILMMA.org

exhaustive but should get you thinking of other things you could do to ensure each client experiences exceptional client service.

1) Institute a 24/7 Client Advocate Hotline.

2) Give clients updates on their case every 30-45 days.

3) Use software that allows clients online access to your case management system so they can check the status of their case.

4) Send out client surveys every 90 days asking how things are going and how they believe their case is being treated.

5) Create scripts for your staff to use when they are confronted with certain questions and situations.

6) Institute mystery caller services to ensure your intakes are being handled professionally. Chris Mullins at Mullins Media offers an excellent service (see: www.mullinsmediagroup.com)

7) Base attorney and staff bonuses on survey results of their clients.

8) Use benchmarks to ensure cases are being moved off point and do not languish. Remember, cases are not like wine – they do not get better with age.

As stated above, these are just a few suggestions. You can come up with many more depending on the experience you are trying to create.

Strategy #5 – Start a Newsletter: Increase Referrals and New Clients

A regular newsletter done properly can double your referrals in around 10-14 months. The newsletter must be done at least every other month to be effective. You want to make sure the newsletters are printed and not digital. You can do both, but if you only do one or the other, do the printed version. Printed newsletters are 50% more effective than digital newsletters. Go back and review the direct mail chapter and also check out www.newslettersite.com for a more thorough explanation of the most effective way to create a quality newsletter that will double your referrals.

Strategy #6 – Create a Niche Practice

You cannot be all things to all people. To compete with the mega personal injury law firms, you must hone in and niche a certain practice area just like many doctors have done. For example, it is not enough to be another orthopedic doctor today. If you really want to thrive, you must focus on a sub-niche like orthopedics for the knees or shoulders.

By choosing a niche practice area -- and by limiting the cases you accept to that one or a few practice areas -- you create the impression that you're a specialist. The benefit to your prospective client is that you can get better results for your client than a lawyer who accepts many different types of cases. (Note: If you want to use the term "specialist", make sure you check and comply with your State Bar's rules of professional conduct.)

Below is a list of possible sub-niches you could explore:

- Palsy Cases
- Dog Bites
- Railroad Accidents
- Boating Accidents
- Aviation
- Fallen Merchandise
- Slip and Fall
- Trucking Accidents
- Construction Accidents
- Scaffold Accidents
- Swimming Pool Accidents
- Cruise Ship Accidents
- Inadequate Security
- Motorcycle Accidents
- Bicycle Accidents
- Business Torts

Practical Advice. Proven Solutions.
www.PILMMA.org

- Environmental Torts
- Pharmacy Negligence
- Chiropractor Negligence
- Lawn Mower Accidents
- Heavy Equipment Accidents
- Fire Cases
- Burn Cases
- Mesothelioma
- Attractive Nuisance
- Daycare Negligence
- Sexual Assaults – By Clergy or Teachers
- Legal Malpractice
- Medical Malpractice
- Police Negligence
- Federal Torts
- State Torts
- Nursing Home Negligence
- Electrical Injuries
- Child Cases
- Brain Injuries
- RSD – Reflex Sympathetic Dystrophy Cases
- Auto Wrecks
- Products Liability
- ATV Rollovers
- Defective Air Bags
- Skiing Accidents
- Ski Mobile Accidents
- Bad Faith Cases
- Dram Shop Cases

If you select Dog Bites as your sub-niche, a possible tagline could be, "Dog Bites are what we do and it's all we do!" That is actually a great USP.

Practical Advice. Proven Solutions.
www.PILMMA.org

By sub-niching you have taken two key steps:

1) You have positioned yourself as the expert.

2) You have positioned yourself so you won't have to compete on the same playing field as the mega personal injury firms.

If you follow the 6 strategies above -- and niche yourself deeply into one specific injury practice area -- you will successfully compete with the mega firms long into the 21st century.

What's more, you'll enjoy the personal and professional benefits of being a lawyer -- the benefits that drew you to the practice of law -- the benefits you want and so richly deserve.

Practical Advice. Proven Solutions.
www.PILMMA.org

Appendix A

What Is Education Based Marketing?
By Trey Ryder

You have two choices when you select a marketing message. You can choose selling-based marketing, in which you take on the role of a salesperson and deliver a sales message. Or you can choose Education-Based Marketing, in which you take on the role of a consultant and educate prospective clients about their problems and the solutions you can provide.

Selling-based marketing is built around a selling message, sometimes called a sales pitch. The sales pitch is often delivered using methods that reach out to prospective customers, such as telephone selling, direct mail and door-to-door sales. Education-Based Marketing is built around an educational message, which replaces the sales message. The educational message is commonly delivered to prospective clients through educational means. These include written materials, media publicity (articles and interviews), advertising, seminars, newsletters, audio and video tapes, and Internet websites. Frankly, you can educate your prospective clients using any method through which they can get your information and advice.

Typically, your Education-Based Marketing program works like this: You create an educational message, which you first put into the form of a written handout. Then you offer your handout to prospects who are interested in your services. Prospects call your office to get your free written materials. You respond by sending the materials and inviting prospects to an upcoming seminar. In addition, you keep prospects educated through your educational newsletter.

You put your message in front of your prospects through paid advertising, articles in newspapers and magazines, and interviews on radio and TV. In addition, you communicate with people on your mailing list and invite them to attend your seminar and bring their friends and associates.

Practical Advice. Proven Solutions.
www.PILMMA.org

Selling-based marketing creates these problems:

1. Prospects go out of their way to avoid you because they are tired of selling and sales pressure. They don't like to be approached by salespeople who have something to sell.

2. Prospects don't think they can trust you because all of us have been burned by salespeople who gave us "inaccurate" and even false information in their eagerness to earn a commission.

3. Prospects are defensive and protective because they expect you to try to pressure them into buying something they don't want or need.

Education-Based Marketing provides these solutions:

1. You give prospective clients what they want, information and advice -- and you remove what they don't want, a sales pitch.

2. You maintain your dignity because you never make any effort to sell.

3. You establish yourself as an authority because prospective clients see you as a reliable source of information.

4. You don't seek out prospects; instead, they call you.

5. You reach prospects during the first stage of the decision-making process, often before they call your competitors.

6. You identify even marginal prospects who suffer from phone-call fear, but who aren't afraid to call for your free information.

7. You prove that calling your office is nothing to be afraid of. In fact, it's a positive experience.

8. You save money because you don't need expensive brochures.

9. You receive calls from qualified prospects who are genuinely interested in your services and you screen out people who are not your prospects.

Practical Advice. Proven Solutions.
www.PILMMA.org

10. You establish your credibility and make a positive first impression by offering helpful information rather than a sales pitch.

11. You save time by answering common questions in your materials and seminars, rather than answering the same questions over and over.

12. You begin to earn your prospect's loyalty because you've made an effort to help him, even if he doesn't become your client.

13. You know precisely how well your marketing works because you can count the number of prospects who respond -- and the number who go on to become clients.

14. You gain a competitive advantage simply by using this method because few, if any, of your competitors currently use it.

15. You benefit from the synergy of several educational methods that reinforce each other.

16. You earn a true profit, rather than just creating more work and more overhead.

Now you understand why the American Marketing Association featured this innovative method on the front page of its national publication, MARKETING NEWS. Now I invite you to profit from this unique method.

About Trey Ryder

Trey Ryder is a lawyer marketing consultant that specializes in education based marketing.

For more information about Trey and to learn about the Ryder Method of Education Based Marketing, visit: www.TreyRyder.com

Practical Advice. Proven Solutions.
www.PILMMA.org